DEFIANT JOY!

Carol McLeod

VIP
VISION IMPRINTS PUBLISHING
A Thomas Nelson Company

www.thomasnelson.com
Tulsa, Oklahoma

DEFIANT JOY!
© 2006 by Carol McLeod

Published by Vision Imprints Publishing, Inc.
8801 S. Yale, Suite 410
Tulsa, OK 74137
918-493-1718

Unless otherwise noted, all Scripture quotations are
taken from the *New American Standard Bible* (NASB), ©
1960, 1962, 1963, 1968, 1971, 1972, 1973, 1975, 1977,
1995 by The Lockman Foundation. Used by permission.
Scripture taken from *The Message Bible.* © 1993, 1994, 1995,
1996, 2000, 2001, 2002. Used by permission of NavPress
Publishing Group.

ISBN: 1-599510-19-7
Library of Congress catalog card number: 2006922964

Printed in the United States of America

All of us know that life is a journey through low valleys and high mountain peaks. Carol McLeod has discovered the greatest truth of living life to its fullest is how to handle the difficult times of life with a joy that defies all of our circumstances. *Defiant Joy* is a must for every Christian to truly learn to live above the circumstances of life.

—Bishop Tommy Reid
COVNet churches and The Tabernacle

Carol McLeod exudes joy. I've known this since our college days when she was a friend and mentor to many of us young collegiates. Her joy was contagious and we all loved being with her. Now many years later, after raising her beautiful family and partnering with her pastor husband, Craig, she still exudes that same joy. Here in her book and in her *Just Joy* conferences she has chosen to share her time-tested secrets to strengthening joy with the rest of us.

—Gayle Haggard
Wife of Ted Haggard, President of the National Association of Evangelicals and pastor of New Life Church

Carol McLeod is a beautiful woman of God who I looked to as a mentor in college. Her godly example as a wife, mother, and minister has always been an inspiration to me. She truly is a gift to the body of Christ. You will be enriched and encouraged as you read her latest book, *Defiant Joy!*

—Lisa Osteen Comes
Lakewood Church
Houston, Texas

Lisa Osteen Comes serves as an associate pastor of Lakewood Church, under the leadership of her brother, Pastor Joel Osteen. Her husband Kevin, is the administrator of Lakewood Church, and they have three children—twin girls, Catherine and Caroline, and a son, Christopher.

Carol McLeod is well on her way to becoming one of the nation's top communicators to women.

—Fred Caserta, President
Kingdom Bound Ministries

Carol has captured the essence of what women need to live in peace with God, their families, and themselves.

—Donna Russo, Executive Director
Kingdom Bound Ministries

What a joy reading Carol's insights on life! Carol writes about thought-provoking truths she has learned from her life experiences. Her challenge to the readers is that the only way we are going to live overcoming lives and really be a witness of the love of Jesus is in spending time with God daily in His Word and in prayer, then walking out what we have read.

—Sharon Daugherty
Victory Christian Center
Tulsa, Oklahoma

Dedication

To Craig . . .

The love of my life,
The man of my dreams,
My heart's companion.

"A successful marriage requires falling in love
many times, always with the same person."

I am more in love with you today than I was
on July 31, 1977!

Contents

Acknowledgements

God has a "Hall of Fame" reserved for men and women of God who have chosen to live their lives with great faith. You can read about it in Hebrews chapter eleven. I decided that if God could have a "Hall of Fame"—then so could I! My life is filled with "Hall of Fame" champions who have challenged me to live a life of defiant joy and to run my race with perseverance and determination.

Matt—My firstborn son—you paved the way for the others with such excellence. Now, you are not only my son but also my friend. I love the way you think, the way you live, and the way that you love. Your wisdom never ceases to amaze me—I now come to you for advice!

Emily—You are a perfect fit in every possible way. I couldn't love you any more if I gave birth to you myself! Thank you for loving our Matt and for loving us.

Christopher—When you were little, you said that when you grew up you wanted to be a singer, a soccer player, and a joker. You have grown up to be a man of God, a worship leader, and a record producer. We can never begin to imagine all that God has for you!

Jordan—If there were an award given for the world's greatest teenage boy, you would win it! You have always made my life happier just by being with me. I am going to miss you more than words can say. Keep singing your song.

Joy-Belle—Thank you for living up to your name! When I grow up, I want to be just like you. You are my little girl who has grown up to be my kindred spirit.

Joni Rebecca—Some people say that God always saves the best for last . . . I think that's why we all love you so much! Keep hiding God's Word in your heart because that is the only way to do life. Our family was not complete until you arrived—our piece of heaven on earth!

Mom—I have heard it said that "Home is where your story begins"—if that is true . . . then it all started at 6555 Alleghany Road. Thank you for always believing in me and thinking that I could do anything that I attempted. Thank you for a legacy of joy.

Nanny—What did I do to deserve you? When I married Craig, I never imagined all of the joy that *you* would bring into my life. Thank you for heartfelt prayers and for sharing with me your love of the Word of God.

Sarah—My sister, my daughter, my friend, my disciple— You are bound for greatness in the kingdom of God. Our hearts are truly knit together in love and for that, I am grateful. Thank you for serving me every day and for loving my family.

Julie, Linda, Melissa, and now . . . Alane—What a team we are! Are we really allowed to have this much fun?! I love serving God with the four of you. Thank you for your creativity, your excellence, your stellar attitudes, and your support. I have a feeling that . . . "We Ain't Seen Nothin' Yet!"

Kerri and Kelly—The anointing on your lives makes me reach deeper for the things of God. It is an honor to minister with you—you always put a song of joy in my heart! Thank you to Pete and Jerry for sharing each of you with me.

Pastor Tommy and Wanda Reid—Craig and I are humbled to walk together with you during this incredible season of both of our lives. Thank you for the opportunity of a lifetime and for believing in us.

Mary and Cindy—Your prayers have made a way time after time after time. If there is anything worthwhile in Just Joy ministries, it is because you have loved me enough to pray for me. Your reward will be great.

Carolyn Hogan, Debbie Edwards, Shannon Maitre, Dawn Frink, Marilyn Frebersyser, Donna Russo—Being friends with each one of you has been sheer delight. You all ought to write a book on friendship—it would be a best seller! "Truly great friends are hard to find, difficult to leave, and impossible to forget."

Annie McCune—Thank you for breakfast out . . . for creative ideas . . . for praying for me . . . and for everything else that you do and that you are. I know that our friendship is new . . . but I have a feeling that there are many memories to be made!

Tuesday Evening Ladies' Bible Study—You are my adrenaline! Tuesday night really is the best night of the week, isn't it?! Thank you for lifting me to heaven and allowing me to go to the world.

Just Joy Board of Directors—Thank you for your wisdom, your interest, and your vision. Please keep speaking into my life and staying on your knees!

John Mason—Thank you, from the bottom of my heart, for the opportunity of a lifetime. Life is not measured by how much money you make, how many degrees that you earn, or by the number of stamps in your passport. Life will always be measured by the depth of friendships that one develops. Craig and I are looking forward to continuing a rich and lasting friendship!

Also, with great love and admiration to Ellen Stamps, Evelyn Roberts, Ruth Graham, and Corrie ten Boom. You have given to my generation a heritage of godliness and honor. Thank you for being my role models—my heroines of the faith.

Chapter One

Defiant Joy!

Desperate for Joy!

Honestly, I just don't understand Christians!

Do you understand why some Christians are victorious while others live in constant defeat?

Why do some Christians experience great joy in spite of sorrow while others act like spoiled brats? You may know the spoiled brat group. Someone from this group may be lurking about your life. Nothing makes them happy!

Tell me truthfully, have you figured out why some Christians find deep meaning and purpose in just living their lives daily for Christ? They find pleasure and purpose in changing diapers, taking out the trash, and being a light at work. Yet, there is another disproportionately large group of born-again, blood-bought, filled-with-the-Spirit believers who are caught in a continual maze of "Who am I?" "Where am I?" "Why am I?"

Why are some Christians known for depression, for whining, for complaining, for negativity? You know who I am talking about because you want to hide when you see them walking toward you down the aisle at church! When you see their number on your caller ID—you are just like me—you ignore it! And yet—there are other Christians who are known for their trademark brand of unsinkable joy—their smile lights up every room into which they walk. These contagious Christians laugh often and bend down to talk to children. They make everyone else feel so much more important than themselves.

Why are some Christians determined to walk in victory while others seem to take some warped fulfillment in drama and tragedy? These Christians do not go from glory to glory but from drama to drama and are known by the very fitting, descriptive title, "soap queens."

There are some Christians who find deep contentment in the small, simple blessings of life—the smile of their children, the smell of their husband's aftershave, or having a cup of coffee with a neighbor. There is yet another very large group of Christians who would find absolutely no pleasure in winning the lottery! There would still be something to complain about,

"Well, you know last month I could have won nearly two million dollars more!"

"The government is going to get more than I will!"

"Now I will have every Tom, Dick, and Harry asking me for a handout!"

I want you to have the secret weapon that will allow you to live your life for Christ in the most miraculous of ways! There is a very real, yet easily solved mystery that will enable you to live above and not below your circumstances. There is a key that will unlock the door of your heart to defiant joy!

DEFIANT JOY!

I would like to introduce you to a joy that will literally enable you to defy your circumstances or the "hand that you have been dealt." There is a joy that will take you through every storm, every disappointment, every marital spat, every unpaid bill, and every lonely night. This joy will lift you above your unmet expectations and will give you purpose and meaning in the humdrum of life!

I would like to warn you, however, that this is not an easy way to live. This lifestyle is going to take gut-wrenching determination and relentless discipline. This way to do life is not for the weak, the weary, or the insipid! Wait a minute! What am I talking about?! Of course it is for you—it is especially for you! It is for all of us!

The sad reality is this—only a few of you will choose this way of living. Only a few will choose joy over depression and victory over defeat. Only a handful of believers will have the tenacity to tie themselves to triumph rather than tragedy or trauma.

Before you read another word of this book, let me protect you from wasting your time. Do not read this book if you are not desperate for joy and for the power that it will bring into your life. Do not think that this book is written by a self-help guru or is filled with pop psychology. I hope that you saved your receipt because if you think that this book has the sweetness of a Hallmark card, the fragrance of a bouquet of springtime flowers, or the plasticity of a pasted-on smile then you have my permission and my blessing to get your money back!

This book is about joy that is defiant. It is about how you find that kind of joy, how to embrace that kind of joy, and then how to keep that kind of joy. Some chapters will be painful while others will be rich with deep, biblical insight. Some chapters will cause you to step on your spiritual tiptoes while others will be marked by stark simplicity and raw challenge. If you are desperate for a joy that is defiant, then throw away your receipt and read on! I dare you to choose joy!

CAN YOU AFFORD JOY?

There are at least 150 Scriptures in the Bible that contain the word "joy"! H-m-m-m-m, sounds thematic to me . . . does it to you?! Isaiah tells us that we are to *joyfully* draw water from the wells of salvation (Isaiah 12:3).

Jesus has a well in your yard with your name on it that belongs to you and to no one else. This well in the yard of your life is a deep and healthy well that will never run dry. It is way, way down—in the deepest part of this well—that the secret to defiant joy is found. Most Christians are not willing to dig deeply enough to reach the miraculous spot where His joy is just waiting for them! However, there is a "catch" concerning this well and the catch is this: you have to be willing to pay the price for the water of joy. Although this well is a deep and healthy well that will never run dry—this is one expensive well. Salvation is the only commodity that is free in the kingdom of God. With every other spiritual blessing you must be willing to pay top dollar!

You have to do some hard work to obtain the joy that is waiting for you in the well with your name on it. You have to be willing to sweat and to strain and then to pull and perhaps dig deeply below the surface of your life. Are you willing? Are you desperate enough to pay the price for this joy?

Many women come to me pleading, "Carol! I want to be just like you! I want to face life the way that you do! I want to have the joy that you have!"

If I were truly honest with these desperate housewives, I would respond something like this:

"Do you really?!"

"Do you want to pay the price that I have paid?"

"Do you want to make the hard choices that I have had to make?"

I am not building myself up here . . . there is not one ounce of pretense in my response to these women. I am just telling you the simple truth. There is a price to pay for joy that I am not sure you are willing to afford. Joy costs an astronomical sum and don't fool yourself by assuming that joy is free.

The psalmist says it differently than this but the message is the same, "In His presence is fullness of joy"(Psalm 16:11)! You will find all the joy that you will ever need this side of heaven in His presence. His presence is the payment for joy on earth. Do you have enough of His presence to make a down payment on joy? Or, are you bankrupt when it comes to His enduring presence in your life? Do you stay in His presence long enough to experience defiant joy? Or, like your quiet times, is joy just a little blip on the radar screen of your life?

If you are not reading your Bible every single day of your life, joy will be that illusive butterfly that flits in and out of your world. If you are not on your face before the Lord every day then you will never experience the joy that is pervasive enough to take you through rebellious children, cancer, and bankruptcy. This "on your face" kind of commitment has nothing to do with whether you are Methodist or Charismatic, Baptist or Pentecostal, Episcopalian or Presbyterian. It just means that you are willing to join Abraham, Moses, Jehosophat, David, Daniel, the three boys in the fiery furnace, Hannah, Mary, Elizabeth, Paul, and many others in their desperation to have enough of His presence to make a down payment on joy.

It is all really a choice, isn't it? I am fifty-one years old now—I am quite sure that I have lived at least half of my life! Of this one thing I am certain: I will choose joy! There is no other way to live! I will bask in His presence and stay at His feet. I will become addicted to the Word of God and devour each sweet morsel. I will choose joy. The question remains yet for you to answer: Are you desperate? Are you desperate to do life His way and to choose joy? Will you choose joy? I dare you! I dare you to choose joy!

Chapter Two

What a Gift!

The Joy of His Presence!

Happiness . . . it's just so circumstantial, isn't it? If we can experience something good then we are able to exude happiness.

If things go our way, you know—the bills are paid, the children are behaving, he took the trash out—then we are able to plaster that Cheshire, self-content smile on our faces and just let it shine.

If it's not raining, then it must be sunny, so I'm good.

His mother actually said something nice to me—I think that I will respond with kindness!

I might be single but I have an unbelievable date this weekend so I will buy everyone doughnuts at work today!

What is it about women and their circumstances? We think that we *deserve* to walk on the sunny side of the street and if one tiny, little shadow crosses our pathway all of a sudden our life becomes the frozen wasteland of Siberia.

I am only being human—like you—when I admit that I *love* the happy days of my life so much more than troublesome times. If you were brave enough to be honest you would agree with me that life is much easier lived when there are no clouds hanging out in your blue skies and a raindrop wouldn't even dare to plop in your eye!

A MEMORY BOOK OF JOY

Before our journey into joy begins, let's become acquainted for a few moments. You don't know me well and I don't know you at all, so will you spend a few short paragraphs with me looking through the picture books of our hearts? Let's allow our hearts and minds to return to the times in our lives when we were absolutely filled with the most joy imaginable this side of heaven.

My wedding day! Perhaps the most perfect day that I have ever lived! I will always remember the sweet, redolent smell of gardenias wafting up from my bridal bouquet and the look on my father's face as he walked me down the aisle to give me to the new man in my life. I remember the single tear that gently fell down Daddy's cheek and yet the sparkle of love in his eye as he looked into my groom's face and said, "You better take good care of her. "

If you are a mother, you will never forget the birth of your first child and gazing down into that miraculous face. As you counted the ten tiny fingers and toes, I am certain the tears were pouring down your cheeks unto the baby blanket as you were immersed in the miracle of new life. The smell of a baby—so fresh from heaven and so filled with the potential of God!

Very few days of my life have held the celebratory possibilities of that long-anticipated graduation from college. I remember waiting, with my academic comrades, for our turn to walk into the eight-thousand-seat arena that was filled to the brim with screaming brothers and sisters, proud parents, and camera-holding grandparents. I can vividly recall the professors in their academic regalia preceding our graduating class as the university orchestra played the majestic strains of *Pomp and Circumstance*. I can still remember— nearly twenty-nine years later—looking for my friends in the crowd of mortarboard bearing heads and remembering with great thankfulness this piece of life that we had shared.

Christmas morning—the best day of the year! Wrapping paper flying, twinkling lights on the tree, children's exclamations, Christmas music playing, hugs and kisses spread around liberally. A sweet tiredness is etched upon the faces of the parents as the thrill of watching their children soaks into their souls. This magical morning is only one of a heart full of memories in the picture book of parenting.

Perhaps, like me, your favorite memory of unabashed joy is just one ordinary day planning a picnic in the backyard with the people that you know the best and love the most. Watermelon is dripping down everyone's chin and next on the agenda is the messy, yet sidesplitting, egg toss! The day is sure to end in a hilarious attempt to see who can catch the most fireflies and a family game of hide-and-seek in the summertime twilight.

I'll bet that the memory album of your heart holds hundreds of memories just like mine. Some of our memories are painful while others make life worth living! I love life! I wake up every morning and the first thought that crosses my blonde brain is, "Boy! I sure do love my life!" When I wearily lay my head on the pillow—much too late most nights— my closing thoughts are covered with great thankfulness for a life that just gets better and better every single day.

FORTUNE-TELLERS AND LEG IRONS

Now that we know one another just a little better, I may put the damper on our dewy relationship by submitting to you an entirely outrageous life philosophy. If the aforementioned memories are the only ones that you have had the pleasure to experience, then you are absolutely clueless when it comes to an experiential knowledge of joy. I would like to submit to you that you have not experienced joy until you have been to prison.

Paul and Silas, as they had been many times before, were in the wrong place at the wrong time (Acts 16:16-31). They were going to a place of prayer when a slave girl, who was demon possessed, began to follow them. This girl was actually a fortune-teller, or psychic, and her owners made a fortune by using her for their own gain. She followed Paul and Silas around for many days and was bellowing loudly, "These men work for the King of Kings and the Lord of Lords! They are going to tell you how to be saved!" Paul had finally had enough of the out-spoken, loud, pitiful creature and cast a demon out of her.

The masters of this young diviner were furious because their income disappeared as quickly as the demon did. The outraged owners gave Paul and Silas a thrashing that they would not soon forget and then took them into the center of town to have them arrested. The impassioned crowd in the market square first tore the clothes off Paul and Silas and then proceeded to flail them with rods in public.

This type of treatment is not intrinsic to only first century Christianity but it happens to Christians in the twenty-first century as well. Just as the clothes of Paul and Silas were torn from their backs and they were left standing publicly exposed, many Christians feel the embarrassment of secure coverings being ripped from their life. Perhaps the thing that has been violently torn from your life is your job, or your ability to conceive and bear children, or your marriage. Maybe the circumstance √ that has left you vulnerable in front of the entire world is that your health has radically changed. You thought that you were safe and covered when, without warning, the comforts that brought sanctuary disappeared in one single heartbeat. What has been ripped away from you, just as the clothes of Paul and Silas were torn away, and left you exposed to the elements of a cruel world?

If that weren't enough, after being exposed with no protection to the unkind elements, then life has decided to beat you up! Paul and Silas were not only left standing exposed but were beaten by the inhumane crowd in the town square. Perhaps you can relate to this kind of treatment because your circumstances have mauled every ounce of respectability that you had been clinging to and now, you are bruised emotionally and are bleeding from nearly every pore of your body. It has been year after year after year of no breakthroughs or not enough money. You cannot recall the last time that you claimed a friend who did not turn their back on you. You have experienced nothing but death, destruction, and barrenness and it has become simply too much to bear.

After Paul and Silas had their clothes torn off their very backs and had been beaten beyond recognition, they were thrown into prison and placed under heavy guard. This was not a shining moment in New Testament church history—the leaders of the early church were in prison and there was no way out. This is scandalous fodder for the cover of *The Jerusalem Enquirer!* Paul and Silas, who were once preaching partners, are now cellmates in a Roman jail and their feet have been clamped into leg irons to ensure that there is no hope for escape.

For some of you, the picture that has been painted of Paul and Silas is one that is sadly familiar to you. Not only have you lost your security in life, not only have you been beaten up beyond recognition, but now you have been tossed unceremoniously aside. You are in a situation that smacks of worthlessness and you are sure that there will be no opportunities for significance in your future. Someone has locked up your dreams and thrown away the infamous key. You, like Paul and Silas, are in a deep, dark place and you believe that no one knows that you are in the bowels of despair. Your feet have been locked up and you have no direction in life.

GET THAT SPIDER OFF MY FACE!

A Roman prison was consumed in utter blackness. It was damp in this wretched place down in the belly of the earth that smelled like urine and vomit and human excrement. Rats and spiders made themselves at home on every prisoner's body—but the prisoner was not able to protect himself because his hands and his feet were in chains. A prisoner was served one meal per day that consisted of moldy bread and tepid, dirty water. A Roman prison was a place that quickly gave way to mental illness and it only took a few nights in this place to lose one's mind. Every time that a guard arrived with the decayed meal, he would take the opportunity to kick his prisoner in all the places that were the most tender. A prisoner sat in his own excrement and was never brought clean clothes once he entered the hellacious dungeon. Most prisoners in a Roman prison had not committed a bona fide crime but had merely offended someone of great importance and power. These men and women were not jailed fairly but were victims of a vicious system.

This is the environment in which Paul and Silas were trapped with no date of release in sight. It was at midnight, the very darkest time of the night, when Paul and Silas made a decision of earthly defiance. Midnight is the time when most people are losing hope or giving up in despair or giving in to depression. But, Paul and Silas were not "most people" . . . are you? Are you going to do what *most people* do when their security is gone, when they have been beat up beyond recognition, and when all hopes of significance are shadowed by midnight? Or, will you make a better choice of earthly defiance?

Paul and Silas found joy in the putrid smell of prison and in the dark and damp of hopelessness. Paul and Silas discovered defiant joy with their hands and feet bound in purposelessness and in the sewage of their own existence. Paul and Silas found joy! Have you? Or are you choosing to wallow in the worst of your circumstances and allowing the smell of life to dictate your emotional responses? You have not had the opportunity to experience the joy of heaven until you have been in the hell of prison. As Christians we have a divine duty to meet the very worst that life throws at us with defiant joy!

A HEALTHIER ALTERNATIVE

How can anyone in their right mind consider trials a reason for joy (James 1:2)? James, the disciple, knew that joy was a choice of grand possibility although some might think it absurd or unthinkable. Some people might think that joy in the face of trials is a most ridiculous choice—unless, of course, you know Jesus! That we are to choose joy in situations when joy would, in the natural, be our very last choice is a remarkable command. When we are angry with people or disappointed with life, when we are in the throes of grief or tormented by depression, James points us to the much healthier alternative of joy!

In this verse that almost seems self-contradictive in theory, James encourages the early church to "consider it all joy whenever you encounter various trials" (James 1:2). Chalk it up to joy when things just do not go your way and refuse to allow pain or struggle to rob you of the joy of new growth in your life. Focus on the future benefits of this time of trial rather than on the difficult time in which you find yourself immersed.

Jesus used this very strategy when He was hanging on a Roman cross with the blood dripping from His body and the screams of pain locked inside His heart. Because Jesus knew that joy was just one choice away, He endured the cross and kept His eyes on you (Hebrews 12:2). He set His eyes on you when He was suffering—you must keep your eyes on Him in your moment of excruciating pain.

James teaches trial bearers from all centuries that we are to consider our moments of pain to be moments of pure joy. There should not be one drop of disappointment or depression in the life of a believer because we know the eternal medicinal benefits of genuine rejoicing! When we are in the prison of hopelessness, we know that the only way out is pure and heartfelt worship!

We are called to count every trial that we encounter an opportunity for pure joy. This should happen "whenever," not "if" but "whenever" we encounter different kinds of trials. Trials will happen, I guarantee it! You will encounter a trial if you have been a Christian for more than fifteen minutes. There are unavoidable difficulties in life but you must not ✓ allow them to become "joy robbers." Allow tragedies, inconveniences, unpleasantries, and trials to become "joy reapers" in your life!

Hang onto your seats . . . you better be sitting down . . . I have to remind you of one more thing that James said. He said that there would be "various" trials in your life! Are you screaming yet?! The word "various" implies that there is more than one trial in your life and probably more than one prison in your future.

IT'S TIME TO GROW!

The reason that you are able to consider the adversities and heartbreak of your life as pure joy is because you are about to hit a growth spurt! The testing of your faith is going to produce the endurance of a marathon runner and the strength of steel in your life (James 1:3). Your roots are determined to defy the rocky soil of hardship and find their place in the rich, fertile ground of joy. After you go through this growth spurt, you will no longer be a mini-Christian or a midget in the faith but you are about to experience heroic change in an otherwise ordinary life. Mini-Christians rejoice when they are not going through trials, when their bills are paid, when they receive a good report at a doctor's office, or are the beneficiary of a tax refund from Uncle Sam. But James demands that we, who are destined to grow, consider it pure joy in the very face of trials because we are about to have an extreme life makeover!

James is not encouraging believers to "pretend" to be happy because pretense will get you nowhere. "Rejoicing in trials" leaves "happy" so far back in the distance that it is a pin prick on the journey to joy. Why settle for happy when you can experience joy?! Joy is God-oriented and is not self-oriented or circumstance-centered which is why you need to spend some time in a trial or in a prison to experience defiant joy.

Joy is gut-wrenchingly honest. Joy says, "I hate the smell of this prison but I love the praise and worship music here!"

Joy is 100 percent genuine. Joy reports, "The food is lousy, the rats are unfriendly, and this is no five-star resort but nothing can separate me from the love of God!"

Joy is purposeful. Joy acknowledges, "There is only one way out of this place. Self-pity does not hold the key to the door out nor does depression but I am having the joyride of my life!"

POWERFUL JOURNALISTIC TECHNIQUE

Paul wrote Philippians, one of the shortest epistles in the New Testament, from a Roman prison cell in the murky light of a window. Certainly a man in the cesspool of life should be allowed to write a letter of complaint or vent his emotions or even tell his side of the story. If anyone has the right to be "real," it is a man who is in prison unfairly and it should be legitimate for a prisoner to share his deep disappointment with God and with life and with the hand that he had been dealt.

Paul uses the word "joy" or "rejoicing" fourteen times in this one short, seemingly insignificant letter. He is in prison, for goodness' sake, and he is espousing the benefits of choosing to rejoice. How many times today have you said the word "joy"? How many times in the last year have you chosen joy over the pending depression of your circumstances? We think that a blip of joy on the radar screen of life is worth a standing ovation from all of heaven. We break our arms patting ourselves on the back when we sing even though we had a miserable spat with our husband on the way to church this morning.

You must understand that the joy that comes from being a Christian is pervasive—there is nothing too hard for it to crack through. Joy is perpetual—it never, never stops. Joy is purposeful because it will usher you straight into your destiny.

Paul gave the church at Philippi an amazing recommendation while he was in prison, "Rejoice in the Lord always, and again I will say rejoice!" (Philippians 4:4). What strange advice written by a man in a dank prison cell! Paul is teaching all generations of Christendom that our inner attitudes do not have to reflect our outward circumstances. It is easy to become discouraged about unpleasant circumstances or even to take insignificant events much too seriously. There will always be situations in your life that will cause unhappiness, lack of productivity, and emotional instability but there should never be any event in your life that stifles your ability to rejoice or is able to steal your joy.

It is only possible to embrace a ceaseless song of joy when you are living your life securely *in the Lord*. There is no joy in circumstances but your joy is a result of a vertical point of view. A vertical point of view enables you to sing in prison when you are looking straight up into the face of God. If you have horizontal vision and maintain a minimal view of your life, your situations, and your relationships then you will view a dry and barren wasteland of existence as far as your eyes can see. But, if you choose to look vertically into heaven, then you will have a panoramic view of love, peace, and goodness. If you can live a vertical life rather than a horizontal existence, your life will be one grand symphony of joy. You will no longer have time to complain because you will be utterly consumed with the joy of His presence. You will be so genuinely engrossed in the beauty of praise and worship that the torment of disappointment will have no impact on your life. The word "depression" will be erased from the dictionary of your soul and you will be dancing into your destiny!

A prison will tempt you to live a horizontal life, as will a trial. But I can guarantee that if you live horizontally in prison, you will be eaten alive by the varmints of depression. If you stubbornly remain with your eyes set on the horizontal call of your trial, you will be burned into a charred remnant of your former self. But, if you defiantly choose to live a vertical existence then you will be captured by His joy.

You really do not have a choice but to immediately obey Paul's New Testament commandment that will keep you in a state of defiant joy. Joy is not a spin-off of obedience to God but joy *is* obedience to God. Joy is an act of obedience and we are commanded to rejoice in the Lord and to take unabashed delight in the company of His presence.

"It is a Christian duty for everyone to be as joyful as they can be," said the great twentieth-century theologian, C. S. Lewis. The goal of your life is to glorify God and you do not glorify Him through

31

depression, whining, or complaining. You bring glory to God when you choose to sing at the top of your lungs even though you are locked up tight at the midnight hour in prison.

I wish I had been there in that Roman prison with Paul and Silas and the other prisoners. The time that Paul and Silas spent in prison was marked by two singular activities: praying and singing worship. Now those are my kind of men! Was it fair that they were in prison? Absolutely not! God had actually *verbally* called Paul and Silas on this evangelistic venture when their first stop on the journey landed them in a nightmarish prison. Life is not fair and if you want "fair" you can forget about defiant joy. Life is not fair but God is always good.

The prisoners were listening intently and wholeheartedly to Paul and Silas as they sang. The other prisoners, nearly out of their minds with hunger and inhumane treatment, had never heard songs in the night before this surprising night. They had heard screaming and cursing with gut-wrenching tears in the darkness, but their ears had never before been privy to a melody of joy. The world is listening intently to you, just like they were listening to Paul and Silas while in prison. What are you doing while you are in prison? What are the activities that consume your time while you are bound in chains and are up to your heart in darkness? It is our natural reaction to have a pity party, to give in to depression, to blame others or even God. In prison, it is commonplace to compare your life with others who are currently not spending time in prison. You may be writing letters of complaint to the management, "What did I ever do to deserve to be treated like this?!"

How you respond while in prison will play a major role in how others respond to your Savior. Paul and Silas were bleeding, cold, and bruised and I can guarantee you that they did not "feel" like worshipping. They defied their circumstances while in prison and were determined to give glory to God even in the darkest of times. Their radical response was an act of their will not a result of expressing the way that they felt.

As Paul and Silas lifted their voices and their hearts while in the horrific conditions of prison, a shifting of the earth's surface suddenly began to occur. There was a rumbling, then a shaking, then an earsplitting roar filled the room and opened the prison doors. When you choose to sing rather than sniffle and to praise rather than pontificate, prepare yourself for an earthquake that is going to rock your Richter scale! When you choose joy while in prison, God is ready to move heaven and earth on your behalf. The very foundation of your prison is about to be smashed into thousands of pieces and you will be set free from the chains that have bound you when you choose joy over depression. Not only will you be set free but those around you will be emancipated as well. You may be spending some time in an unjust prison because you *are* the key to open the door for someone else. The act of your will that causes you to rejoice and to keep right on rejoicing is about to loose someone else's prison chains. What an extraordinary possibility!

When the guards who were keeping watch that momentous night realized that the earthquake had loosed the chains of the prisoners, they went into lockdown mode. The guards were responsible for the prisoners and if a prisoner escaped, the guard would either have to serve the escaped prisoner's term or be killed on the spot. Paul assured the prison guard that they were all still there. (I just bet that the reason Paul and Silas were hanging around was so that they could lead all of the prisoners to Jesus Christ!)

When the guard called for a light so that he could scrutinize the situation, he did not realize that he was about to meet the Light of the World. He knew that his need was light but what he did not realize was that the Light that he desired was not of the earthly kind. This Roman prison guard was preparing to walk by faith and not by sight and he would no longer be a victim of darkness and of fear.

Paul and Silas assured the distraught prison guard that all that he needed to do was simply to "believe!"

"Believe in the Lord Jesus and you and your household will be saved" Paul and Silas stated (Acts 16:31).

It still comes down to that—to your simple belief in Jesus Christ. Like Paul and Silas, I believe in Jesus and I believe in the power of joy. I believe that when I choose to rejoice, I am ushering in the presence of Christ into every prison in which I find myself. I know that prison doors are miraculously opened in the presence of Jesus. You may not see Him with your natural eye but He has most assuredly given you the gift of His presence as you walk through all of the dark places of life.

Your feet might be in stocks—but your heart is in heaven! Your body may be beat up and bruised—but your hands are lifted wildly in the air! You might smell like vomit—but your prayers are a fragrant offering to the Lord! You might be at the midnight hour of your life—but you have found the Light of the World!

You and I have a responsibility, a divine duty, to honor the Lord with a lifetime pursuit of the joy of His presence. I must not be small minded enough that I choose to live my life horizontally. A lifestyle of joy and rejoicing is the only way out—will you take the way out that He has given to you? Or will you stay locked up in the prison of your soul? I choose to defy my prisons—to clear my throat and prepare to sing at the top of my earthbound lungs: I WILL CHOOSE JOY!

Chapter Three

The Discipline of Desperation

A Commitment to the Word of God

Our two oldest sons celebrate their birthdays just a few weeks after Christmas. When they were little boys, they were the only grandchildren on both sides of the family—the first of the next generation of world changers! With doting grandparents, an assorted handful of generous aunts and uncles not to mention good-hearted church people, my sons experienced what I like to call "embarrassing abundance"! By February 1st of nearly every preschool year, my home could rival any toy store in America! We had Tonka trucks, Care Bears, Legos, books to last until college, more videos then our local video store, footballs, baseballs, basketballs, games, puzzles, and even a short-lived hamster!!

One year, early in February, just days after their prolific birthdays, my future men of God were bored and fighting. Their brotherly kindness turned into a full-blown feud that would have made the Hatfields and the McCoys hoot with glee! As I looked at the colossal remains of Christmas and birthdays and then heard their voices raised in discontent and frustration, I marched into their pale blue bedroom determined to take care of this situation.

I spoke out of inexperience when I nearly shouted in their little faces, "Honestly, I have given you the world! What will make you happy?"

Christopher, my three-year-old, looked at me from his shock of unruly blonde curly hair and said with tears in his blue eyes, "You make me happy, Mama!"

We are victims of embarrassing abundance as well. I wonder if God ever wants to say to us, "I have given you the world! What will make you happy?"

How will you respond if that is His heartfelt question to you, the object of His creation? Do you merely want more stuff—a more expensive house, a newer model car, a better vacation, more money to spend?

I hope that I will look at Him from the chaos of my unruly life and respond, "You make me happy, God. Your Word makes me happy."

DON'T YELL AT THE KIDS, KICK THE DOG, OR GIVE YOUR HUSBAND THE SILENT TREATMENT!

The Word of God explains exactly how to live and is explicit in the counsel that it abundantly gives. I have discovered that if I want my life to be filled with joy, I must live by His game plan. I must spend time in the Word of God and then obey the strategies of life that are so clearly outlined for His children in the Bible. I absolutely cannot do life *my way* and expect *His joy!* I must not yell at the kids, give my husband the silent treatment, and kick the dog if I expect the blessing of His joy in everyday life. However, I will never learn those practical lessons of life unless I am daily spending time in the Word of God.

Every day, I must make a counseling appointment with the Great Counselor and then I must *take His advice.* Can you even imagine spending massive amounts of money for the purpose of seeing one of the most well-respected counselors in the medical profession and then not taking his or her advice? It would be absolutely preposterous! However, that is exactly what many Christians have the tendency to do when we go to church, hear the Word of God taught with great wisdom, and then go home and wallow in our emotional preferences. When I read the Word of God—and yet continue to give in to anger and unforgiveness—it would be tantamount to telling God that I know better than He does! Who can even imagine such pretentious behavior?

Take God's advice that is found in the Word of God and then thank Him for His advice! You should be so filled with the wisdom and wonder that is found in the Word of God that literally in the night you find yourself awakened by the power of a well-loved Scripture verse.

What do you dream about? I can guarantee you that many of your nightly dreams are the result of the stuff with which you have filled your life. Do you dream about having a new husband? Someone who never snores, always takes out the trash, and wouldn't think of having a midlife crisis! Or do you dream about long, leisurely trips to the mall with an abundance of cash and a body that fits into size ten dresses? Do you dream of exotic vacations in faraway places where the sun always shines and you never have to cook another pot of macaroni and cheese as long as you live? Do you dream about your first love? Perhaps your dream life is filled with pictures of perfect little babies yet to be born whose noses never run and who never learn to say the word "NO!" Or maybe you nostalgically dream of young adults that used to be your babies.

My life should be so centered upon the Word of God that I actually dream Scripture verses. The counsel that is found in the Bible should consume both my waking and my sleeping hours and should be as familiar to me as my home address. God gives infinitely wise counsel in the Word of God and then He confirms it in the night hours (Psalm 16:7).

There is no way around it—if you want to experience the pure and defiant joy that is His will for your life—you will never experience it apart from having a daily quiet time. Joy will always play hide-and-seek with you if you are not spending time with Him in the Word of God every day of your life. If you woke up breathing this morning, you should spend a delightful and glorious time basking in the counsel that is found in the Bible.

WHAT'S YOUR EXCUSE?

There are many and varying excuses that women can conjure up to explain the reasons for not having a daily quiet time. Not one excuse that I have ever heard has impressed me as having any spiritual validity at all. They are all simply what their definition implies: excuses.

The first excuse that many Christian women try to hide behind is this, "I don't know where to start!" Starting is actually the easy part . . . my problem is I don't know where to stop! Allow me to give you some practical suggestions that will pop the air out of your excuse-filled balloon.

Start by reading in the Gospels if your heart's desire is to learn more about the incredible life of Jesus Christ our Savior. That's right . . . start in Matthew and then go on to Mark, Luke, and John. I also particularly enjoy reading a Proverb for every day of the month. On the first day of each month, I read Proverbs chapter one and on the second day of the month, I read Proverbs chapter two. Every month, I read the entire book of Proverbs and then go back to the beginning again. One of the values of approaching the book of Proverbs in this manner is that, as a woman, I end every month by reading Proverbs chapter thirty-one, which is a tribute to a godly woman.

I also find myself captivated by reading at least one Psalm a day. Many days, I find that I have spent more time in the book of Psalms than I have spent in front of the mirror! Those are without a doubt the most blessed and the most profitable days of my life. The days that I lose track of time while reading the Word of God bring utter contentment and joy into a life that can sometimes fall into the trap of cultural expectations.

Excuse number two many times starts with these disturbing words, "You don't understand how busy I am! I am too busy to have a quiet time!" Those heartbreaking words are another recurring excuse that women use to explain their lack of ability to make the commitment to daily time in the Word of God. Many Christians have deluded themselves into thinking that reading the Bible every Sunday afternoon is all it takes to turn them into super Christians. They justify this ill thought-out excuse by quickly adding addendums concerning jobs, kids, appointments, commitments, marriage, the gym, nail salons, school, and the like. I will agree with you on one part of this excuse—*I don't understand!* I don't understand how anything at all could be of more paramount importance than the Word of God in your life. I *don't* understand why women crowd out the power that is found in the Word with flimsy, worn-out excuses.

One practical suggestion that has brought life-time continuity and direction to my journey in the Word of God is that I journal my journey. I buy a journal in which I record what I read every day and the verses that particularly seem to touch my heart. I write questions concerning particular verses or phrases that I do not completely understand. Having a devotional journal brings a practicality to reading and then digesting the truths found in the Word of God. Writing significant verses in my journal helps me to remember the beauty of the Word and then to commit it to heart.

A HIGH-POWER SECURITY SYSTEM!

Have you realized yet that sin will always steal your joy? The devil tries to convince you that sin is going to make you happy—just remember that he is, after all, the father of all lies. Sin will not make you happy—it will make you miserable! We must devise a strategy that will ensure us of resounding victory over sin *every single time!* God has given us His Word as the way to escape the enticement of sin. The psalmist boldly proclaims: "Thy Word have I hid in my heart that I might not sin against Thee" (Psalm 119:11).

I found defiant joy when I realized that memorizing Scriptures was not just for children in Sunday school! This strategy, of Scripture memorization, also vitalized me to have power over sins that had wrapped me up in their vise-like grip. When I started, as an adult, to memorize at least one Scripture every week, suddenly I realized that I was not battling with the sins of the flesh that had tormented me for so many years. No longer did I default to worry when a situation was out of my control because a Scripture would come alive in my heart and I began to trust rather than to worry! Negative thinking and a critical spirit melted faster than the Wicked Witch of the West because my mind was being washed by the Word of God!

If you have the Word of God in your heart, you have a high-power security system that is guaranteed to keep out any sin that threatens to steal your joy. If you struggle with bulimia, or overspending, or anger try this prescription: Read your Bible every day! You need to be more addicted to the Word of God than you are to your sin. I challenge you to memorize at least one Scripture a week and you will be amazed at the freedom that you miraculously experience from sin that has strangled you for years!

A SPIT-SHINE!

It had been raining for days and finally I saw the sun peaking out from behind the welcome springtime clouds! Being a stay-at-home mom with three preschoolers, I was thrilled that I could finally send the children outside. I was preparing my three youngest children, plus my favorite niece, to attend a well-deserved birthday party this sunny morning and couldn't wait to walk out the front door for a breath of fresh air.

I started the task by dressing the oldest ones first and then sending them outside to sit on the front porch while I finished with the younger ones. Jordan, my five-year-old son, looked adorable with his blonde, curly hair and new white tennis shoes. Taylor, my sweet niece who had just turned four, had on black patent leather shoes and white ruffled socks. I warned the two older ones not to move off the porch because it was still very muddy in the yard. The third child out the front door was Joy, my three-year-old angel, who was always trying to keep Jordan and Taylor out of trouble.

I finally walked out the front door about ten minutes later holding the baby, Joni. But to my great dismay, there were no children sitting on the front porch. As I walked around the corner of my house, I saw Joy standing on the edge of the driveway with tears streaming down her cherubic little cheeks, "I told them not to go to the swing set, Mommy! I told them!"

Joy, because she had stayed on the driveway, had just a smidgen of mud on her shoes that I knew I could quickly clean with a paper towel. Jordan, however, had ventured further and let's just suffice it to say that those brand new white tennis shoes were now a thing of the past! He was in to mud nearly up to his ankles. Taylor, the ringleader in all of this, had already arrived at the swing set. Her shoes had become stuck in the mud and now she was wading in water in those lovely white ruffled socks. She had apparently fallen down in the swampy mess and was covered from head to toe!

We never made it to the birthday party that day, but the children all learned a lesson in obedience that was not soon forgotten. I had to throw away two pairs of shoes that had been ruined in the morning's mud bath. After the discipline, tears, and baths were over, we had a lovely picnic on the front porch and this time, no one dared escape!

Ephesians chapter five teaches us that the Word has cleansing power in our lives. When you are spending time in the Word of God on a daily basis, you will be washed clean of the drudge that is in your life. Some of you have been wallowing in the mud for far too long and it is time to spend hours and hours under the blast of His shower. You will be cleaned from the inside out and won't miss the party that He has planned just for you!

How long have you been in the mud? How deeply have you been in the mud? Perhaps you need to memorize more than just one Scripture a week—you need to spend hours in the cleansing power of the Bible. The Word of God will literally put a "spit-shine" on your life. It has the power to clean out bad attitudes, to wipe your life clean of depression, and to obliterate negativity faster than you can say, "Dial Soap"!

THE CARTOGRAPHY OF THE WORD

In the ancient world, most people wore flimsy, poorly constructed sandals. This footwear was generally made of leather and had a strip that came up between the first two toes. Attached to this leather strip was a small tin cup that could hold about a tablespoon of oil. At night, when walking was required, there were no street lamps to light the way or no brightly shining lights from windows. It was necessary to set flame to the oil in the tin cup on the sandals so that the night traveler could see where to place his next step. The tin cup cast a glow of about twelve to eighteen inches in front of the traveler's foot to protect the traveler from stepping on rocks, tripping on the roots of trees, or stepping on scorpions. This light became all that was necessary for safety in the most treacherous of routes.

The psalmist tells us that God's Word is a lamp unto our feet and a light unto our pathway. God's Word will cast a glow in your dark and treacherous journey that will give you direction and keep you from harm. The Word of God will highlight the best route to take and will also warn what roads will lead to devastating destruction. The powerful Word of God will give wisdom to you and will help you to think more clearly.

When my husband, Craig, and I are preparing for a trip, he likes to believe that he is a direct descendent of Christopher Columbus and maps out our route as if his life depended upon it. He usually buys a new map, because we cannot find the one that we bought last year, and agonizes over exactly what routes on which we will be driving. Sometimes, he will even contact AAA and have them send us a map that has the best route highlighted and also warns of roads that are under construction or ill-advised.

The Bible is our road map to life and we must follow the route that God has so carefully highlighted for us! We must take His advice and not travel on the roads that lead to destruction. We do not have a better idea than God does—our lives are only well lived when we follow His directions.

A DIVINE WORKOUT SESSION

Many of us go through life worn-out, beat-up, and just plain tired from fighting all of the time! We are out of breath, out of shape, and weary from the relentless dogging of our circumstances. Have I got news for you! Watching Oprah will not strengthen you and Dr. Phil has no power to help you change your life! There is only one avenue that will take you to a lifestyle of strength and power and that one way is by reading the Word of God every single day that you are breathing.

David, the psalmist, knew this principle well and he begged God to "Strengthen me according to Your Word" (Psalm 119:28)! The Word of God is better than any workout session and it will wield results in your life that will enable you to face all that life throws your way with power and strength. Our goal is not natural strength that will give us the power to fight with human tactics but rather our passion is supernatural strength that comes directly from time spent in the eternal Word of God and will empower us to fight with the resources of the capacity of heaven!

Americans are such a predictable bunch of people—we want everything to be instant and easy. Every year, right at the beginning of January, there is an absolute mad dash to join gyms, the YMCA, or to hire the services of a personal trainer. Where are those same people in mid-March? Right where they were in December—sitting on the coach, eating junk food, and thinking how their clothes have magically shrunk! If things are not easy or instant, we automatically think that it is not worth the effort that it entails and then we give up and hightail it back to where there were no demands placed on our precious little lives.

The principle of strength training is the same in the natural world as it is in the supernatural world. To become a person of power takes time and it is something that you must work at consistently to experience persistent power. Exercise does not change your out-of-shape figure the first day or the second day that you discipline yourself but after a month or two of a daily, rigorous work-out, you will begin to notice some differences. It is the same way in our quest for strength from the Word of God—this is not some magical fix in which you only read one verse every forty-seven days and expect to be Super Christian! It takes a daily commitment to enjoying the Word of God and to hiding it deeply within your heart. You can easily lose what you have gained in supernatural strength if you are not consistent in this Christian discipline. When you spend time reading God's Word every single day, it will empower you to be more than you can be on your own and to do more than you are humanly able to do!

PUT UP YOUR DUKES!

I hate confrontation of any kind at all! I don't like it when Craig and I have a "discussion" or when I have to sit beside one of my children and gently remind them of the principles that our family has chosen to live by. I want life to be easy and for everyone to get along! I love to think that my world is surrounded by a little white picket fence with flowers happily growing along the edge of my life. I hate fighting of any kind and beg God not to ask me to confront people!

I thought that when Craig and I were married, we were going to have the perfect marriage. In my fairy-tale mind, I just knew that he would always take out the trash and that I would never nag. I believed with my whole heart that he would understand all of my emotions and that I would never give him the silent treatment! It only took about ten days of marriage for both of us to realize that our battle technique needed improving!

As Christians, we should never resort to the human mode of hand-to-hand conflict. For those of you who are married, how do you respond after having yet another marital spat? Or, maybe you are not married but are in the middle of World War III with someone at work or with a saint at church. Do you give this person the silent treatment and continue to ignore them day after day? Or maybe you are not the silent treatment type of woman, instead you scream! Or perhaps you forage through the pantry and find all of last year's Christmas chocolate and go on a chocolate binge. Maybe you call your mom and complain, or worse yet, maybe you call your best friend and rant and rage. Some of you do none of the above but you sure have a blast going out and spending a lot of money to make yourself feel better.

Those are all rotten ways to fight! Your battle technique needs improving *immediately*. The book of Ephesians explains that "the Word of God is the sword of the Spirit"(Ephesians 6:17). When you are in the Word of God consistently you will no longer feel the urge to give in to the human tendencies even though you find yourself in the middle of a battle. The Word of God is an indispensable weapon at your daily disposal and owns the inherent power to disarm all of your enemies. In the midst of conflict of any kind you must go to the Word of God for wisdom, for battle technique, and to find the best route to peace.

The Bible clearly teaches us that it is more blessed to give than to receive. It also instructs us that when we give, we will receive back more than we have given! If you are in a financial battle, you must obey the Word of God when it emphatically teaches that God will bless givers. Your way out of a financial hardship is to be a giver not a taker.

If you are in a relationship battle, you must not give the silent treatment to that person, you must not give in to gossip, and you must not call names or speak in anger. The Bible says that we are to bless our enemies and to love those that hate us. Your battle strategy for a complete victory in every relationship skirmish is to bless the other person and to show extravagant love. The Word always wins!

MOST LIKELY TO BE BLESSED!

We all love to talk about blessing and favor and abundance—that is part of being a Christian that causes our spiritual adrenaline to soar in anticipation! Do you know how to ensure that you will be a blessed Christian and that you will walk in the favor and abundance of the Lord? It's a four-letter word: the W-O-R-D!

The psalmist, David, actually says that there is no way to measure the blessing of those who walk according to the Word of God and who observe His commandments. In Psalm 119, David poses the rhetorical question, *"How blessed* are those whose way is blameless, who walk in the law of the Lord?!"* How blessed are they? How blessed are the ones who choose to love the Word of God and to do life according to His commandments? There is no way to measure that kind of blessing (Psalm 119: 1-2)!

David also exclaims in the same Psalm that he rejoices more in the way of the testimonies of the Lord than in the blessing of riches and wealth. Would you rather have a quiet time today or win the lottery? You will be more blessed by loving the Word of God than if perchance you purchase the winning lottery ticket! When you read the Bible, it brings more blessing and favor your way than a retirement account or a bonus check (Psalm 119:14)!

The truths found in Psalm 119 are endless in their encouragement that there is a way to favor and blessing. A sure and certain road to blessing beyond measure is found in the powerful Word of God! David says that when you search for favor with your whole heart—you will find it in the graciousness of the Word. David, a shepherd boy who became King, knew the secret to blessing was found in the words that came straight from the throne room of God almighty (Psalm 119:58)!

WITH A SONG IN YOUR HEART!

The Word of God will change you from the inside out and will do more for your fragile emotional state than a miracle drug, an appointment with your psychiatrist, or the opportunity to be on *Who Wants to Be a Millionaire?* The Word of God is not magic—but it is miraculous and it will cause the most depressed heart to be glad and sing for joy (Psalm 119:9)! You will not be able to explain it, you may not understand it, but where there used to be darkness there will suddenly be a song. The pain and sorrow of a lifetime of disappointment will absolutely be erased with a spirit of rejoicing. The Word of God will ensure the joy that defies all of your life's circumstances! I guarantee it!

Chapter Four

Petticoats or Power Tools?!

Did you have your nails done this week? Or maybe you spent money at the mall. Did you send a load of clothes to the dry cleaners or have your hair done? Perhaps you treated yourself to a pedicure or decided to be totally extravagant and went to the tanning salon. Did you buy new makeup or go to the gym in hopes of taming your cellulite?

Let me ask you just a few culturally sensitive questions: How long do you spend getting ready in the morning? How long does it take you to be presentable from the time that your feet hit the floor until you are ready to greet someone at your front door?

I have sadly learned that my feminine life in the twenty-first century can be merely about pretense if I am not careful. Looking good, smelling great, and keeping up with Hollywood can consume way too many hours of my life if I am not aware of purposeful living. America is the only nation in the Western world in which women have to be a size eight to be considered beautiful. We spend a dizzying number of hours and an exorbitant percentage of our paychecks at the mall in order to try on, examine, and then buy a temporary piece of fabric that will wear out or go out of style by next year at this time.

Life to a Christian woman must be so much more than this—if you are desperate for defiant joy, that is! Your life must not be about pretense, appearance, or petticoats if you desire to face life with defiant joy. If your strategy for dealing with the disappointments of your culture is to purchase a new outfit then the result of this sad strategy will be continual defeat. If you try to soothe the deadlines of busyness by getting your nails done then you will be eternally frustrated. If you try to inject hope into the despair of your low self-esteem by darkening up your pale skin, then you will live never knowing His power in your life. It's true, you will look good and receive a few well-placed compliments. You might even win a second glance or two but you must realize that there is not power in appearance. Power comes from preparation!

THE FEW, THE PROUD, THE ROMAN ARMY!

Paul was spending undeserved time in a Roman prison . . . again. His only crime was that of loving the Lord too dearly for an earthbound existence. His passion for Jesus Christ was the driving force behind every word that he spoke, every decision that he made, and every place that he went. The world never has understood that kind of living and probably never will. Paul spent an inordinate amount of time in the man-made dungeons of his day while his spirit was soaring in the liberty of Christ-based living.

There was never enough food in prison nor was there enough light to effectively write down all of Paul's bursting revelations while in confinement. His wrists were rubbed raw by the tight metal bands that joined him to the Roman soldier who had been chosen to guard this man who was judged to be a threat to society. The soldier's job description was simple: make sure that Paul did not have the opportunity to escape. Paul's job description was unmistakable: to share the gospel of Jesus Christ with this military warden.

"Where are you from?" Paul may have asked mildly one evening after spending just a few hours in prison.

"What's it to you?" was perhaps the response of the burly man who had been trained to guard his heart with military propriety.

"Just wondered . . . that's all," was Paul's humble response.

Paul kept a submissive attitude in his attempts to build a relationship with this man who was known as one of Rome's finest. After days of innocent attempts to socialize with this disciplined man, Paul was finally able to gently goad him into talking about his training.

"I was a young boy when I was chosen to join the ranks of the finest fighting force in the world. When I first entered military duty, I had no idea that my training would be so thorough and so challenging."

"Tell me some of the ways in which you have been trained to defend your nation," Paul might have astutely asked.

"I have been taught not only to fight but also to ensure the safety of the entire Roman nation even during times of peace. I am an architect, an engineer, and a cartographer. I have been trained medically so that I can take care of my wounded comrades. Some of my brothers in the Roman military are able to build and maintain the finest network of roads that the world has ever known. They say that all roads do lead to Rome, you know," responded the man of strength and valor.

"I have heard that you are the most disciplined men ever to have lived," inserted Paul, "and that many battles that you have won are due to relentless courage and staying power. Is it true?"

"It is all true!" boasted the soldier. "The Roman Army is unconquerable thanks to bodily discipline and hard, efficient training. A Roman soldier is able to learn new battle tactics faster than any other soldier on the face of the earth."

"Tell me about the armor that you are wearing," Paul continued. "I am interested in every piece of armament that you are wearing. What is the purpose of each?"

Could it be that Paul peppered this grenadier with calculating questions? Is it possible that Paul even used this opportunity to investigate the heart and mind of his well-trained guard and then translated what he learned to a spiritual application that echoes through the centuries?

"Well, first of all, you must wear the full armor for total preparation . . ."

THE EXCLAMATION
POINT OF CHRISTIAN LIVING!

"Finally, be strong in the Lord and in the strength of His might," is the battle call that comes from the heart of Paul straight into our twenty-first century weakness (Ephesians 6:10). Paul vibrantly proclaims that the most important character trait which we are to embrace is the virtue of strength! Paul is thoroughly convinced that the exclamation point of Christian living is God's mighty power changing the very way that we approach life. God's will for your life is that you would be divinely strong and it is His plan to infuse you with His very own strength. When you decide to be a defiantly joyful Christian, you will find yourself miraculously strong! "The joy of the Lord is your strength" (Nehemiah 8:10)!

The devil is not after your marriage, your health, or your finances. Old slew foot could care less about your children, your home, or your ministry. What Satan wants is your joy and he is relentless in using all sorts of techniques to steal this valuable commodity from your life. The manner in which Satan tries to steal your joy is by going after your marriage, your health, your finances, your children, and anything else that you hold dear. But what he really cannot wait to get his greedy little hands on is your joy. Why? Because he knows that it is your joy that makes you strong! If Satan can steal your joy, he will turn you into a weak, whining, ineffective Christian. God has given you His joy because He wants you to be strong and to be filled with the power of His might!

If you were to hire a personal trainer, this trainer would give you an exercise program that would increase the strength in your muscles. However, what a personal trainer cannot do is to take his or her strength and transfer it to you. Only God can do that! The power that God gives is "dunamis" power and it is miraculous power. Dunamis power gives you the ability—with an abundance of might—to work a miracle! It was dunamis power that raised Christ from the dead and it is that very same power that God transfers to you! You have the capacity for dunamis power in your life when you steadfastly refuse to allow the devil to steal your joy! What an exciting possibility!

Paul calls us, in these verses from Ephesians, to a perpetual lifestyle of strength! "Be strong" is a continual verb tense that has no beginning and no ending. It is a ceaseless and unremitting strength that comes from God's infusion of dunamis power into your life.

DRESSING FOR POWER

After Paul calls us to God's weight room, because that is the place where we find His power, Paul then begins to instruct us in exactly what we are to wear. This is a fashion show of the best kind—it never goes out of style and you will be dressed not for success but for joy and for power! Now that sounds like my kind of wardrobe!

God has provided an incredible wardrobe that will enable you to go through life as prepared for power as that Roman soldier whom Paul spent time with in prison. The wardrobe has been selected and is purchased . . . it is guaranteed to fit well and make you look your absolute best! However, you must decide to put it on. Will you put it on? Or will the full armor of God dry rot in your spiritual closet? Maybe you will be cautious in your choices and will only wear one piece at a time. Your goal as a man or woman of faith is to fight well and to fight strong. Your goal is not to merely look good or to make a grand first impression—your entire life should be about embracing the power that He has abundantly given to you! God's armor is the only armor that will guarantee a victorious Christian life full of joy and power. It really does not matter what color you have on, if your roots need some attention this week, or if you have a chipped nail! What matters is that you emphatically put on the full armor of God and fight all of your battles with His strategies.

Honestly, when was the last time that you actually won a battle with your tongue? Or by lashing out with your emotions? When was the last time that you experienced victory by going on a spending spree or an eating binge after a disappointment in life? Does backing your husband into a dusty corner really make you feel more powerful? Is worry really your way out of the stress of life?

You will only walk in triumph when you fight with His battle strategies and you will only experience defiant joy when you forgive rather than condemn or gossip. You will see the light at the end of the tunnel when you pray rather than pronounce your emotional superiority. It is self-control that gently takes you by the hand and helps you deal with disappointments and it is heartfelt praise that will lead you into triumphant living! You are only more than a conqueror when you pray for and when you give to and when you bless the people who have wronged you (Romans 8:37).

You are fully competent in the heavenlies to bring decisive victory upon the earth. We are engaged in an authentic battle—it is not pretend nor is it imagined. The good news is that we have the resources not only to fight but to conquer over-whelmingly when we put on the full armor of God and leave it on!

"Put on the full armor of God so that you will be able to stand firm against the schemes of the devil" (Ephesians 6:11). Before you can move ahead and take back territories from the devil, you must first *stand firm*. This is a word picture not of a march or of an assault but of holding the fortress of your soul for the Heavenly King. When we stand, dressed in the wardrobe that He has provided for us and in the power of His strategies, we are standing in no ordinary geographical position. He allows us to stand in His presence even while here on earth and gives us great joy for the battle (Jude 1:24)!

Since the beginning of recorded time, the devil has been known as a slanderer, an accuser, and a liar. The devil's goal for your life is to do every single thing that he can to berate and demean you so that you will see yourself as less than significant. Satan wants you to be less than a conqueror while God calls you to be more than a conqueror! The "father of all lies" schemes against you so that you will walk in daily, heart-breaking defeat but the Bible says that when you follow Christ, He always will lead you into tremendous triumph (2 Corinthians 2:14)!

You have a responsibility to ensure that God's will for your life unfolds in certainty. You *must* keep your armor on . . . otherwise you are fresh meat for Satan!

You are strong in the Lord and in the miraculous function of His dunamis power. You have put on the full armor of God and have purposed to fight His way and not your way. Now, it is time to identify your enemy (Ephesians 6:12).

OL' TOOTHLESS

The identification of an enemy is the only way to create an effective battle strategy. If you think that your enemy is something or someone that it is not, you will have no chance of winning your battles. Your husband is not your enemy nor is your mother-in-law. A bad doctor's report is not your enemy nor is your checkbook, your creditors, or the girl in the drive-through window who never gets your order straight! Your children are not the enemy and neither is your boss or your cantankerous neighbor. Your enemy is the accuser of the brethren himself! Look him straight in the face and realize that he is a toothless lion that can merely roar but not bite. Satan only has force—he has no power! Not only is he powerless, but he is completely unable to tell the truth. Every single word that he speaks to you is an outright lie and is worthy of no further attention from you!

The highway to heaven is strewn with the wreckage of Christians who never were able to discover how to combat the wicked one and his fiery darts. These wasted skeletons, disintegrated from warriors into wimps who thought that ethical wisdom or watching *Dr. Phil* or earning more money would help them win their life's battles. These cadavers of Christianity embraced social justice rather than mercy, self-help books rather than the Bible, and recreation rather than revelation. These powerless carcasses fought their battles with educational prowess and sadly thought that life was "all about me." When you fight your battles with good intentions rather than with the wisdom found in the Word of God you might as well go into battle fighting naked!

I know . . . I know . . . all of this battle talk is too much for some of you lily-white Christians who only sing to organ accompaniment. Your battle technique consists of picking daisies while tra-la-la-ing down life's yellow brick road and placing your fragrant flowers in the barrel of Satan's gun. Have I got news for you! The day that you became a Christian is the very day that you became a warrior! You are in the army now!

In this passage from Ephesians chapter six, concerning the full armor of God, there are two specific verbs that apply to spiritual warfare. The first verb is to "stand firm against" (verse 11) and the second verb tells us to "resist" (verse 13). These verbs do not imply a battle technique of all-out military combat, but like the Roman army, persuade us that sometimes vigorously opposing one's enemy comes down to simply standing one's ground. The bravest way to resist the devil may be to stand face-to-face and nose-to-nose against the adversary in a position of relentless determination.

GETTYSBURG

"Therefore, take up the full armor of God so that you will be able to resist in the evil day, and having done everything to stand firm" (Ephesians 6:13).

Not only do these timeless verses tell us *how* to fight our battles, they also tell us *when* to fight our battles. We are to stand firm and to resist *in the evil day.*

Have you ever noticed that some days are just harder than others? Some days are mere skirmishes, when after subduing a minor assailant, you are able to stand up, brush yourself off, and start all over again. Mothers of teenagers and two-year-olds know this for certain! Other days can be a veritable Gettysburg in the life of any Christian—these days are filled with immense fatalities and the blood is flowing deeply. Ask a woman who has been through a broken marriage or the death of a child and she will tell you that she has lived through Gettysburg.

I have a dear friend who is beautiful, well educated, and highly successful. Nadine's world revolves around corporate intrigue, political gains and losses, and economic power plays. She is filled with wisdom and self-assurance and yet knows Whom she serves. Many women look at Nadine's income bracket, her crowded passport, and her powerful position with great envy. However, Nadine looks at my world of laundry that never ends, teenagers who are always hungry, and the perpetually broken basketball goal in my yard with longing. She has never married and wonders, "If only. . . ."

One day as Nadine and I were catching up on our busy lives lived in different kingdoms, the tears started to pour down her lovely cheeks. She explained that she had to fire someone that week and the challenge had taken its toll on her emotionally. The man whom she had fired was caught looking at pornography on his corporate computer. Nadine had to walk into his office, watched as he packed up only personal possessions, and then escorted him with a security guard to the front door. Nadine had to tell this father of three, including a newborn baby, that he could never set foot on the property again and that there would be no severance package. Some days are just harder than others.

As Nadine and I prayed together and I shared with her these verses from Ephesians, we realized that her strategy was not an earthly one but a heavenly one. She called her former colleague that night from her home phone and invited him and his family to church. She stopped by his house that weekend with a home-cooked meal and a Christian book concerning addictions. Nadine quietly inserted that she knew the name of a Christian counselor and would be happy to babysit if the couple needed some time alone. The couple now attends church and sits in the third row holding hands.

How do you fight your battles? With anger and outrage? With emotional superiority and ethical coldness? Or do you find a way to bring the love of

Christ into the battle zone? Are you standing firm in the principles of Christ and His mercy that knows no end? Will you make a difference in your war-torn world or will you conduct business as usual?

CLOTHING OF CHARACTER

Paul now lists the specific parts of the full armor of God and the order in which we are to put them on. First of all, Paul tells Christians, from all centuries, that you are to "gird your loins with truth"(Ephesians 6:14). You can snicker all you would like but let me gently remind you that to a man, his loins are the most sensitive part of his anatomy. It is also the part of a man's biological structure that begets life. This part of one's body needs protection, otherwise there will always be excruciating emotional pain and your life will cease with you because you will lack the ability to stir up new life. If you do not surround your life with His truth, you will have no influence on the generations to come (Ephesians 6:14).

Men actually wore skirts in ancient Rome and when in battle they took a piece of sturdy fabric and brought it up between their legs for further protection and for freedom of movement. This is what truth does for you: It protects you from severe emotional pain and then it gives life to you and enables you to beget life!

Truth starts with knowing Jesus because He is the Way, *the Truth*, and the Life (John 14:6). Jesus also emphatically taught that when we know the Truth, it is then that we are truly set free (John 8:32)! Knowing the Truth, which only comes from knowing Jesus, will give you a freedom of movement that you have never before known. You will be set free from sin, from compromise, and from emotional pain. To remain totally free, you must stay in the Word of God because His Word is truth (Psalm 119:142)!

The next particular item of the armor of God that we are to put on is the "breastplate of righteousness" (Ephesians 6:14). A soldier's breastplate protected his vital organs from the piercing weapons of the enemy. Righteousness protects your vitality as well. Righteousness is living life God's way and ridding your life of the compromise of your culture. As Christians who long to make a difference in the world today, we are to abstain not just from doing evil but from all appearance of evil as well (1 Thessalonians 5:22)! It is enormously important to allow righteousness to guide you in all of your choices in life. *Your emotions will tell you want you want, your culture will tell you what is acceptable, but righteousness will lead you into all truth!* When you live a life of righteousness, which is, of course, based on the truth found in the Word of God, you will be protected from the weapons of the enemy. If, on the other hand, you take down your guard of righteousness, you will be wounded, perhaps mortally. The first time that you enter into moral compromise, it might only be a flesh wound or a disappointment or a minor setback. But, the next time, it will be easier to compromise truth and righteousness because you will think, "Well, last time I compromised there was no permanent damage done. It must be OK."

If you continue to compromise the righteous lifestyle found in the Word of God, soon God will take you off the front lines because He does not want you to be killed! To neglect what we know to be wholehearted commitment to righteous choices is to leave a gaping hole in our armor. When a woman is clothed in righteousness, she is shielded and secure and nothing or no one can touch her! Righteous women are always filled with the joy that comes from the freedom of His will and His ways. "You have loved righteousness and hated wickedness; Therefore God, Your God, has anointed you with the oil of joy above your fellows" (Psalm 45:7).

IT'S ALL ABOUT THE SHOES!

Early in his military career, a Roman soldier was unmistakably convinced of the high value of sturdy sandals. Durable, well-made sandals protected a soldier's feet from the elements of the geographical terrain and from injury. Sandals enabled a soldier to move ahead quickly and to outdistance the enemy. Military footwear boasted iron hobnails protruding through the sole of the sandal for extra grip on mountainous terrain and for the rocky, Roman soil. The hobnails on the bottom of the sandals were also used against the enemy in hand-to-hand combat. No Roman soldier went into battle without his multipurpose footwear.

You are a soldier, whether you like it or not, and the day of impractical, flimsy, toe-pinching footwear is over for you! "Shod your feet with the preparation of the gospel of peace" (Ephesians 6:15).

This verse in Scripture is one of the heavenly oxymorons in which I have come to take unabashed delight. It is certainly a divine contradiction that as soldiers in the army of Christ, we are trained to prepare ourselves for warfare with peace! What a spiritual irony that the weapon of warfare in the heavenlies is the gospel of peace on earth! This gospel of peace will enable you to move ahead in life and will give you sure footing in a mountainous world with which you are not familiar. The gospel of peace will provide for you a way where otherwise you could not go on your own and will help you fight off the enemy in hand-to-hand combat!

You should be ready at any moment, in any situation without a second thought to take out the gospel of peace and allow the Word of God to fight all of your battles for you. "Counselors of peace have great joy" (Proverbs 12:20)!

DON'T GO INTO BATTLE WITHOUT IT!

One of the dirtiest fighting methods during the days of the Roman Empire was the tactic when an enemy would take bits of cloth and then would wrap them in pitch or tar. These mini-missiles were set on fire and sent spiraling through the air. This tactic of flying flaming bullets was a nuisance and they were able to instigate much harm. These small, yet ferocious, flaming darts caused many an army to retreat.

The Roman Army developed the impenetrable shield, which guaranteed that the flaming darts of the enemy would not do their dirty job. The shield was a piece of leather or canvas stretched across a wooden frame and then was treated with first-century flame retardant. All of a sudden, the obnoxious technique of spiraling, flaming balls was rendered useless.

Your enemy is throwing fiery darts left and right at you and his goal is to send great travesty into your life and to cause you to retreat. The darts that we experience are people's arrow-like tongues, pieces of impurity from our culture, selfishness, doubt, fear, and perhaps disappointment over the hand that life has dealt to us. These things are much more than a nuisance and have the capacity to burn and destroy marriages, relationships, and churches. The only way to combat these pieces of flying fire is to lift your shield of faith high into the air and extinguish each miniscule missile before any permanent damage is done.

Please do not think that faith is some deep spiritual treatise that only learned men and women with seventeen letters behind their name are able to understand! Faith is simply this: *Knowing that God is Who He says He is and that He will do what He says that He will do*! That is Faith with a capital "F"! The Bible tells us that without faith it is impossible to please God. I can assure you that it is also impossible to go through life without being tortured by the enemy unless you embrace a lifestyle of faith with reckless abandon!

The opposite of faith is a whining, negative attitude that embraces each form of torture that Satan sends into your life.

"Why me, Lord?"

"She is your favorite!"

"Nothing ever goes right for me!"

"I am just waiting for the other shoe to drop!"

It is time, it is past time, to shut up in the natural and shout out in the supernatural, "God is Who He says He is and He is well able to do what He says He can do!" Faith not only will protect you, but faith actually has the power to extinguish the fiery darts that Satan has ferociously sent into your life. Your faith will put out the darts and then his dirty little fighting tactics will no longer have any power in your life!

You will experience great joy when you put up your shield of faith because there is always joy unspeakable when you realize that it is God Who is fighting your battles for you and that He always wins! That is something to rejoice about (Philippians 1:25)!

IT'S NOT ABOUT LOOKING GOOD . . . IT'S ABOUT BEING GREAT!

If you really want to look your best and dress yourself in a wardrobe that enables you to grab attention, this might be a good place for you to close the book. The next piece of indispensable fighting gear that Paul describes is just plain ugly. A Roman Army helmet had hinged cheek pieces that would smear your makeup and a neck protector that is sure to ruin any wardrobe continuity that you have going on! The helmet was heavy as well as smelly and was guaranteed to smash any great hairstyle instantly! If you really want to live a life of purpose and not of pretense then you will eagerly place the helmet of salvation on your cheap, pretentious attempts at beauty. The helmet of salvation makes a bold statement to your world, "I am His and He is mine! I am dressed in grand style!"

The helmet of salvation is in its determined position in order to protect your mind. Every battle that you will face in life begins in your mind and becomes a mental tug-of-war that you enter into with your emotions and finally with Satan himself.

"She doesn't like me . . . she never has liked me. What a poor excuse for a pastor's wife! I think that I will just leave this church!"

"I bet I won't get a raise this year. I have worked so hard but I am underappreciated here. No one in this entire corporation cares about me. I am being discriminated against!"

"My husband does not understand me. All he cares about is football and Fox News. Why did I ever marry him in the first place? I should have listened to my mother!"

"I have had a horrible day. I was stuck in traffic for twenty minutes, the girl in the drive-through got my order wrong, and all of my clothes have shrunk at the drycleaner's! I think that I will eat an entire candy bar tonight!"

The power that is found in salvation and in a personal, intimate relationship with Jesus Christ will protect your mind. You will no longer have time for the mental skirmishes that Satan sends your way because you will be exploding into praise and worship every chance that you get!

When you have on your military headgear, it will take you to new places of joy! "Restore me to the joy of your salvation" (Psalm 51:12)! Joy and salvation are like Siamese twins—they travel together throughout all of life!

IT'S AN OFFENSIVE VICTORY!

Paul has presented an entire wardrobe of military wear that will help to defend against an onslaught of the enemy. Now, however, it is time to go on the offensive and wipe out the entire enemy army with one simple choice: Read your Bible!

"And take up the Sword of the Spirit which is the Word of God" (Ephesians 6:17)! The Word will be fighting and winning every battle that enters your life. You will never be able to proactively fight, but you will only defend, without the Word of God. The Holy Spirit's primary vehicle for warfare is the Word of God. When God speaks, actions occur! Mountains tremble! Ferocious enemies will run scared with their tails between their trembling legs when they are confronted with the Word of God! Every time that you open your Bible the realm of darkness parts wide open and His truth comes shining through! Satan is rendered powerless when you read your Bible.

Oliver Cromwell was Commander in Chief of all of England's troops during the massive Civil War of the seventeenth century. His entire army was required to fight with a sword in one hand and the Bible in the other hand. Cromwell consistently attributed his military successes to the will of God and the Word of God.

Always remember the truth that is found in the book of Hebrews: "The Word of God is quick and powerful and sharper than a two-edged sword" (Hebrews 4:12). A two-edged sword was a new fighting weapon in ancient Rome and was popular because it did twice the damage of a normal sword. A two-edged sword wounded on both sides of the blade and was able to render inestimable damage both going in and coming out of the flesh. The soldiers were taught to turn the blade as they withdrew it from the flesh of the enemy so that it would make a four-way gash.

The Word of God is more powerful than you realize so you must use it as the most strategic fighting weapon that you have! The Word of God gives you power when you obey its truths. We are a people called to love our enemies—not look for ways to get even with them! It is an intrinsic part of our Christian nature to pray and not to worry, to bless and not to curse, to give and not to take!

When you receive the Word of God into your life and use it to overcome the tribulations that you face, you will experience the joy of His presence in expansive ways! The Holy Spirit will increase your capacity for joy as you embrace the sword of the Spirit, which is the Word of God (1 Thessalonians 1:6)!

Chapter Five

You've Got to Fight for It!

The Warfare of Worship

Let me admit it . . . I am an American history buff and look forward with great anticipation to any and all movies which reenact a piece of history in epic proportions. I have seen them all—*Gone With the Wind, Pearl Harbor, Saving Private Ryan, A Call to Arms*—and am moved to tears as I realize the price that was paid for freedom. Let me assure you, before your blood pressure begins to rise, that I am cognitively aware of the ratings on these movies. 'Nuff said from this history buff!

A true classic, *The Patriot* is an eminently compelling movie concerning the Revolutionary War in America. There is a striking battle scene in this movie in which the British, or Redcoats, march in strict formation. They were wearing their historically famous bright, red jackets as they marched visibly out in the open firing their muskets with precision. The Patriots, or Americans, on the other hand, hid behind trees while dressed in the drab, plain colors of homespun. Blending in with their surroundings, they became the experts of the surprise attack. The Patriots won the Revolutionary

War although they were outnumbered, undereducated, and barely prepared for a war of this magnitude. The British should have easily dominated the ragtag bunch of soldiers who would one day be known as our forefathers. *The Patriots won because the Redcoats did not know how to fight in the New World.* The British were fighting with Old World strategies and outdated traditional military technique.

Many of us, like the Redcoats, fight with Old World strategies but each of us is a brand new person in Christ and we should know better! The old way of fighting no longer works in the New World! We must fight all of our battles as a Christian motivated by the Word of God and not as a person confined to mere mortal strategy. We can no longer afford to fight with our emotions, our tongues, or even our intellect and expect to win.

STRATEGIC CHRISTIANITY

You must be a strategic Christian if you want to live a life filled with defiant joy! It is time to make wise decisions based upon a predetermined strategy of living. You cannot afford to "fly by the seat of your pants" or merely hope for the best. Closing your eyes and wishing on the brightest star in your nighttime sky is of little or no help. You cannot even depend upon the time-honored technique of making a list of pros and cons or flipping that infamous coin! If you can learn to make strategic decisions it just might change the course of the rest of your life! You must decide ahead of time how you will act in times of disappointment, of worry, of weariness, and of battle.

The goal of any battle is to win and to emerge as the champion! The goal of every battle is to dominate in all respects and not just hang on for the win by the skin of your teeth. There is a battle strategy that will ensure your destiny as a champion time after time after time.

A battle, in the life of a Christian, is any situation or circumstance in your life in which the devil is trying to win an evil victory and God is going to turn it for good. It is the classic struggle of good versus evil and you are stuck smack dab in the middle! The book of Genesis describes a battle this way, "But as for you, you meant evil against me but God meant it for good" (Genesis 50:20).

We should become well acquainted with this position because as long as we live this side of heaven we are engaged in warfare and are living our lives for His glory in the battle zone.

Most women turn quite squeamish at the very mention of the casualties of war, military strategy, or the bloodshed that occurs in combat. That is exactly why this chapter was written just for you! If you approach the battles of life in the manner that God has planned—you will never experience emotional casualties or bloodshed! If you fight your battles God's way, your battlefield will become a grand display of praise and worship.

MISERY INTO A MINISTRY

After Craig and I gave birth to two precious little boys, I knew that I wanted more children. We were eager to have a large family and to raise a whole crowd of children that would have the potential to be world changers. When Matthew was four and Christopher was two, we were thrilled when I became pregnant quickly and easily. This pregnancy ended in miscarriage when I was about twelve weeks pregnant and we were more than heart-broken. However, we determined to forge ahead in our heart's desire to have more children and I became pregnant four more times, but each pregnancy would end between twelve and twenty weeks in the pregnancy. Finally, after years of testing, prodding, and probing the doctors at Duke Infertility Clinic deciphered my problem and we were excited to be going full steam ahead with another pregnancy. However, this time, I could not get pregnant for literally months on end!

Finally, after being loaded with fertility drugs to allow me to be able to conceive and then taking the high-powered drug, progesterone, to ensure a viable pregnancy, we gave birth to our miraculous third son, Jordan! Being the selfish person that I am, I decided that my three sons were not nearly enough children and I began to ask God for more babies. This time, the fertility drugs did not work, and my doctors were concerned about what the massive amounts of drugs would do to my system. They encouraged me to be content with my three boys and to give my system a break from the high doses of drugs that I had been taking for years. Craig and I were in absolute agreement with this strategy and went home to raise our three bois-terous, bouncing boys. The very next month, I was nauseous and tired and could not wait to tell those brilliant men at Duke University that what they could not correct God did! I was pregnant with our little girl, Carolyn Joy. When "Joy-Belle" was nearly three, I found myself surprised by heaven again and Joni Rebecca remains the best surprise that we have ever received.

When I was going through the season of infertility and miscarriages in my life, I was in a battle. The devil was out to kill, steal, and destroy but God was teaching me how to be a woman of faith and a woman of prayer. It was the plan of God to turn my misery into a ministry and now my heart beats with the passion of ministering to women who are bruised in the battle zone of barrenness. I love laying hands on women who have not been able to conceive and then nine months later seeing the pictures of the miracle babies that God has sent special delivery from heaven. I love hearing, after prayer, how God has miraculously opened the doors of adoption that have been closed for years and years.

It was the plan of Satan to cripple me emotionally and leave me disappointed and disillusioned. God wanted me to become a valiant warrior on the battlefield of infertility and to teach and train other women how to deal with this wretched enemy. I found joy in my battles because I was overwhelmed with His presence in the battle. What a strange place to find joy! The reason that joy is found in an infinite degree while in the battle zone is because the weapon of our warfare is worship. We worship Him while the darts are flying and the battle is raging. We praise Jesus while the cannons are blasting and all around is in devastation. We do not worship because we get our own way or because we see lovely flowers in full array around our life. We do not praise because we are ethereally happy or because life is just a bowl of cherries. We praise Him because of Who He is and because of our boundless love for Him in all circumstances of life. When your battlefield becomes a full-blown worship service, you will finally know the joy of His presence!

We all have battles whether our names are Billy Graham, Joyce Meyer, or Mary Smith. Your battle might be with someone who lives in your very home or it might be with your finances or your health or with someone with whom you work. You might be battling with a dream or a destiny or the timing of God in your life. It is the ploy of the devil to destroy your battle technique. He wants you to come out in the old fighting mode so he can destroy you. If you have the correct fighting technique, then Satan does not stand a chance.

THE "D" WORD

The devil has three basic strategies that he tries to convince you will work in your life. First, Satan attempts to convince you that depression is a winning strategy. The devil tries to steal your joy so that you lose all of your strength. His goal is to make you so sad and so weak that you are no longer able to stand.

When a circumstance comes your way in the battle zone that causes you to become depressed, you will be in that famous lose-lose situation and will literally be fighting with death itself. If you try to fight your battles with depression, you will tragically discover that depression is not a weapon of warfare but a weapon of spiritual suicide. If you are looking at your circumstances, and not looking at Jesus, you will be depressed. The Bible tells us to stand firm in the faith, to act like adults and to be strong (1 Corinthians 16:13). You can only respond to a battle in this biblical way when you are determined to hold on to your joy and then tell depression where to go!

THE "B" WORD

The second strategy that Satan will try to convince you that will help you to fight your battles is bitterness. Bitterness is depression that turns into angry resignation that things will never change. When you become bitter, you will conjure up a false view of God and will think that He is someone that He is not. Our God is a good God and you are His favorite child; you must always remember that! It is His will to bless you and to bring you into a season of favor.

If you embrace bitterness rather than joy, you will lose your direction in life and will walk straight into the enemy's camp. Bitterness will cause you to be a wanderer with no certain path on which to walk (Isaiah 38:15). Bitterness is not a weapon of warfare but is self-inflicted venom that will kill you quickly. As Christians, we are exhorted to run away from bitterness because when you become bitter, you do not stand a chance on the battlefield of life (Ephesians 4:31).

Bitterness will cause you to blame someone else for your troubles and you will forget how to forgive! Let bygones be bygones and choose a resounding strategy for victory by choosing to forgive. Bitterness and forgiveness are mutually exclusive because you cannot have both in your life at the same time. Always remember that forgiveness is when the *innocent* person allows the *guilty* person to be set free. You will soon find out that forgiveness does not change your past but it will change your future!

THE "ME" WORD

The third technique that the devil tries to convince you that will work is demanding your own way. This is an extremely popular technique in the Western world of the twenty-first century.

How do you act when you don't get your own way? Do you look out only for number one?

Do you resolutely declare, "It's all about me!"

Some people just simply say, "I deserve this!"

Other people, especially women, think that they have to say every single thing that they think, feel, and believe. "Let me tell you how I feel" becomes a sickeningly important verbiage in our vocabulary. We place way too much emphasis on our feelings and our emotions are highly overrated.

Proverbs instructs us that living a life of pride is akin to living a life of destruction and failure. There is no long-term reward for puffing out your chest, demanding your own way, and prancing around like an emotional buffoon (Proverbs 16:18-19).

If depression is spiritual suicide and bitterness is self-inflicted venom, then pride, or demanding my own way, is as sure a death as the kamikaze pilots at Pearl Harbor. You will give new meaning to the phrase, "crash and burn."

The sad thing about this third technique is that you may win a skirmish or two that will serve to boost your self-confidence but you will ultimately be soundly defeated. The battle is not about you, you don't deserve anything and your feelings are going to change by tomorrow anyway! The battle is about His power, His goodness, His faithfulness, and your choice to praise Him while the bullets fly and the cannons roar.

God's principles never change year after year, decade after decade, century after century. His strategy remains the same in the face of cultural disintegration, moral upheaval, and know-it-all people.

There is a familiar story found in 2 Chronicles 20 that has literally changed the way that I fight my battles. I love this challenging piece of history so much that my Bible falls open to these pages. I can assure you with great confidence that what you will learn from this factual account has the potential of revolutionizing the way that you do life.

ONCE UPON A TIME

Once upon a time, in a land far, far away, there was a kind, young king who loved God with his whole heart. He was well employed in reforming his kingdom, providing for justice, and encouraging his people to fear God. His heart's desire was that his kingdom would be comprised of citizens who served God wholeheartedly. King Jehosophat built friendships with the neighboring kingdoms and freely gave food and supplies out of his abundance. He fought for and protected these kingdoms that he had come to call "my friends." "Judah" was the name of the land that was ruled by Jehosophat and it was aptly named because the very name "Judah" means praise and worship. Jehosophat loved his land dearly and tried to help the people of his kingdom live up their glorious name.

King Jehosophat was taken totally by surprise when he was warned that his peaceful kingdom was about to be invaded by enemies from countries far away.

"Jehosophat received this intelligence report: 'A huge force is on its way from beyond the Dead Sea to fight you. There's not time to waste!'" (2 Chronicles 20:2 The Message Bible).

When Jehosophat learned that these enemy forces had freely traveled through the countries with which he had enjoyed friendship, he was heart-broken.

"This surely isn't fair, is it God? Why would the very people upon whom I have showered blessings allow the enemies to march through their territories without even a fight? I have taken such care to show kindness to the neighboring kingdoms and now they have betrayed me as well as the people of this land. What am I to do, God?" (2 Chronicles 20:3).

Jehosophat was filled with fear for his people, his kingdom, and himself. However, rather than allowing himself to become paralyzed by this grip-ping emotion, Jehosophat knew exactly what to do—he turned himself to seek the Lord. Jehosophat spent no time with bitterness because he knew that bitterness would distract him from being able to focus on victory. Jehosophat did not embrace depres-sion even though he was shaken and afraid. Jehosophat knew that fear was not a sin as long as it caused him to turn toward the Lord of Hosts. Jehosophat set his face toward heaven and resolved in his heart to worship God no matter who the enemy was and no matter where the enemy had come from.

"I am determined to follow You, God and to honor You all of the days of my life! I will not allow these sordid enemies, who are coming at me from all sides, to deny me a view of heaven," was his heart-felt cry. "I know that because I am seeking You, I am sure to find You even in this contrary situation."

Jehosophat decided to call an immediate fast and made a proclamation throughout the entire land. The people began arriving from the outlying areas of the kingdom and gathered together in the safest place of all—the house of the Lord.

Jehosophat remembered, when as a little boy, he was taught the words that King Solomon had spoken when the temple of God was completed, "Now My eyes will be open and My ears will be attentive to the prayer offered in this place. For now I have chosen and consecrated this house that My Name may be there forever, and My eyes and My heart will be there perpetually" (2 Chronicles 7:15-16).

Jehosophat believed that the key to this victory against the enemies coming toward Judah would be found in the house of the Lord. He knew that the presence of God was found in the temple in abundance!

"God promised His people that He would be especially attentive when we gather in His house and call on His Name. I believe that God, our God, is listening even now. His eyes and His heart are turned toward us in this place. I believe in the promise of God," Jehosophat exhorted the ministers of his kingdom. "Now is not the time to stand in fear —now is the time to stand in faith!"

Jehosophat stood in the house of the Lord with the entire citizenship of Judah around him. As Jehosophat stood in that holy place, he began to feel the joy of God's presence and began to pray a battle prayer that resounds through the ages:

> *O God, God of our ancestors, are you not God in heaven above and ruler of all kingdoms below? You hold all power and might in your fist—no one stands a chance against you! And didn't you make the natives of this land leave as you brought your people Israel in, turning it over permanently to your people Israel, the descendants of Abraham your friend? They have lived here and built a holy house of worship to honor you, saying, "When the worst happens—whether war or flood or disease or famine—and we take our place before this Temple (we know you are personally present in this place) and pray out our pain and trouble, we know that you will listen and give victory." And now it has happened: men from Ammon, Moab and Mount Seir have shown up. You didn't let Israel touch them when we got here at first—we detoured around them and didn't lay a hand on them. And now they've come to kick us out of the country you gave us. O dear God, won't you take care of them? We're helpless before this vandal horde ready to attack us. We don't know what to do, we're looking to you!*
>
> 2 Chronicles 20:6-12 (The Message Bible)

After bearing his very soul before God and the people of God, Jehosophat stood in the house with the people of Judah in breathless anticipation. The enemy was drawing closer by the moment and the thunder of the approaching stampede could be heard in the distance. Jehosophat looked over his beloved citizens as old men embraced their wives, possibly for the last time. Mothers, with tears streaming down their faces, were holding their infant children and whispering sweet murmurings into their little ears. Fathers were caressing the older children and reminding them of God's saving power.

"Are we going to be slaughtered?" the thoughts were running rampant through everyone's mind. The men were silently begging God not to allow the vicious troops to rape their daughters. The hearts of the women turned toward their homes that they had left in disarray. Would their homes be looted and burned?

Suddenly, there was some movement at the front of the sanctuary. Who was that standing up? Why, it was Jahaziel! The descendant of Asaph who was one of the finest worship leaders in all of Israel! Although Jahaziel was six generations removed from Asaph, the family blessing was still evident in extraordinary ways! Jahaziel had been taught to sing while just a child and had brought new life and meaning into the family Psalms. What was he doing? Was he about to sing?

"Attention everyone—all of you from out of town, all you from Jerusalem, and you King Jehosophat—God's word!" The voice of Jahaziel, son of Zechariah, son of Benaiah, son of Jeiel, son of

Mattaniah, the Levit of the sons of Asaph, resounded through the temple of God.

God was speaking? God had a message for this group of desperate people?

"S-h-h-h-h! Listen, everyone, listen!" commanded the king.

> *Don't be afraid; don't pay any mind to this vandal horde. This is God's war, not yours. Tomorrow you'll go after them, see, they're already on their way up the slopes of Ziz; you'll meet them at the end of the ravine near the wilderness of Jeruel. You won't have to lift a hand in this battle; just stand firm. Judah and Jerusalem, and watch God's saving work for you take shape. Don't be afraid, don't waver. March out boldly tomorrow—God is with you.*
>
> 2 Chronicles 20: 14-17 (The Message Bible)

A mighty roar of victory went up throughout the entire sanctuary! God had spoken in their midst—all was well! All was miraculously well! Jahaziel had been given supernatural intelligence from heavenly sources and the questions had been settled. God's plan was now in place—they could sleep in sweet and confident peace.

Jehosophat quietly bowed his head in the house of the Lord and waited for the crowd to quiet their joyful noise. As the people of Judah watched their king, he lowered himself in front of the altar and knelt humbly before his King. Then, simply he bowed yet lower, and placed his face on the ground. All of the inhabitants of this great nation, men, women, and children fell on their faces and began to worship the Lord. This was a holy moment in the history of God's people—a hush fell in the sacred room as all of heaven held its collective breath.

Jehosophat knew that he had obeyed the God Whom he loved so dearly. He had sought God in the terror of the moment; he called a holy fast for the people of the kingdom and then had led them into the sanctuary. They had prayed in God's house and then listened as God spoke His mighty strategy for sure and certain triumph! Jehosophat had fallen on his face before the Lord of Hosts and now—what was left to do? What was the next step in the victory parade?

"Let's sing!" shouted King Jehosophat. "Let's shout and proclaim our praise to the Lord God of Israel!"

The entire citizenship of Judah and Jerusalem rose to their feet and began to praise *with a very loud voice*. The sound of rejoicing grew in the sanctuary— where there used to be crying and groaning—now there were only songs of joy and shouts of assured victory!

The next morning, after the deep and satisfying sleep of a people at peace, they could hardly wait to approach the battlefield. The anticipation was great as the praise and worship team, dressed in their dancing clothes, joyfully led the way. All followed in ranks behind as they hooted and hollered their way into biblical prominence. They sang because they were not afraid! They praised because they were not depressed! They were able to worship because they were not bitter! They danced into battle because they were not demanding their own way!

It was then that something incredible began to happen—suddenly the enemy troops began to fight against one another. Moabites were killing Ammonites who were slaughtering those from Mount Seir. The Meunites, who had come from Mount Seir, began to rise up against the Moabites until raw confusion turned the battle into a quagmire of an embarrassing bloodbath. The people of Judah stood high on the mountaintop and watched in utter amazement at the incredulity of the foolishness of humanity. Mothers began to shield the eyes of their sons and daughters from the panoramic view of blood, severed limbs, rolling heads, and broken bodies. Every single enemy soldier had been brutally murdered! The people of Judah, once again, began to sing!

King Jehosophat and the men of the kingdom went into the valley to take the spoil from the dead bodies. It took three entire days, from dawn until dusk, for the men of Judah to gather up the food, the weapons, clothes, and precious jewelry that was left among the corpses. The kingdom of Judah had not been destroyed—they had been blessed because they had fought their battle in obedience to God.

On the fourth day following the battle, King Jehosophat gathered his citizenship in the valley of Beracah and they began to bless the Lord from that very spot.

"Let's change the name of this place!" shouted one member of the king's court. "Let's not call it Beracah any longer after today . . . let's rename it the "Valley of Blessing" because this is the place where we have been blessed by our God!"

Jehosophat then led all the men of Judah and Jerusalem back to Jerusalem—an exuberant parade. God had given them joyful relief from their enemies! They entered Jerusalem and came to The Temple of God with all the instruments of the band playing. When the surrounding kingdoms got word that God had fought Israel's enemies, the fear of God descended on them. Jehosophat heard no more from them; as long as Jehosophat reigned— peace reigned.

2 Chronicles 20:27-30 (The Message Bible)

DESTINED FOR VICTORY AND JOY!

Sometimes life just isn't fair, is it? You are living life the right way, doing the right thing, when bam! You feel that you are being attacked from every direction! King Jehosophat was attacked by the enemy forces of the Meunites, the Ammonites, and the Moabites. Who is your enemy?

Who are the "ites" in your life? Are you attacked by depression or by a checkbook that has never been balanced your entire adult life? Are you tormented by unrelenting physical problems or by rebellious children or by people who hurt you? Maybe your enemy is the "other woman" or bad habits that you just cannot seem to conquer. All of these "ites" are formidable enemies.

You will suffer surprise attacks in your life just as Jehosophat did in his kingdom. You will be driving along in your sweet pink Cadillac when all of a sudden, out of nowhere, you are blindsided by a circumstance that threatens to steal your joy. Why are we so surprised when life is not fair or when we do not get our own way? The Bible warns that we should not be surprised when a fiery ordeal comes upon us but that we should rejoice in these very times (1 Peter 4:12-13)!

When fear came upon Jehosophat, he *"turned his attention to seek the Lord."* Fear is not a sin as long as it causes you to turn and seek the Lord and not to focus on your circumstances. If you fixate on your circumstances, fear will cause you to whine and eventually you will be paralyzed emotionally. But fear that causes you to turn in faith is good fear! So Jehosophat "set himself to seek the Lord" which means that he put his face toward heaven and resolved in his heart to worship God in this matter. Jehosophat was a determined man and not even his enemies could deny him a view of heaven. You can be sure that whenever you seek, you will also find (Matthew 7:8) and Jehosophat found the Lord in this contrary situation.

After Jehosophat made the determination that he was going to set his face toward the Lord, he fasted and called on all of his people to fast as well. This is outstanding advice for you—when you see an enemy coming it is a great time to call a fast! This is warfare and one of the most important battlements that you have on your side is fasting. Do not be taken off guard and lose precious time in depression, in bitterness, or in pride. We are human beings made of flesh and blood, but men and women of God from all generations have learned that it just never works to fight the world's way. Fasting is a powerful weapon that is easily able to demolish your enemy's corrupt camp. Do not waste your time in depression —you are too valuable to the kingdom of Christ and to the battle in which you find yourself. If you do not set yourself to seek the Lord and then call a fast, I can guarantee you these three things will happen to you: You will be depressed, you will become bitter, and you will experience the failure of pride.

Jehosophat lived in the very land whose name was synonymous with praise and yet he still had to fight battles. Living in the land of praise had taught Jeshosophat to seek help from the Lord and not from his best friend or from Oprah! Jehosophat did not open the latest edition of *Warfare Today*, he did not start a petition against "ites," nor did he gossip or even go for counseling. Jehosophat called *all* of the cities of Judah to seek the Lord and you need to call every area of your life to seek the Lord as well. Hold nothing back as you prepare to fight the battle of your life. Bring everything that you have and everything that you are and lay it at the feet of Jesus Christ. One of the greatest tools of deception of the enemy is not only to make war with you but also to convince you fight your battles carnally. This will never work—it did not work in Jehosophat's day and it will certainly not work today.

THE POWER OF THE HOUSE

Jeshosophat and the entire country of Judah then stood in the house of God. When you are facing a battle in your life, do not let it take you out of the house of God. Stay in church no matter what is going on in your life. Do not stay home because you are too tired, too depressed, or too weary. Go to church and experience the presence of God with the people of God!

Jehosophat and his people not only went to the house of God but they *stood* in the house of God. The Bible tells us that if we do not have firm faith, we will not stand firm (Isaiah 7:9). You must stand in the house of God and then fight your battles with faith! Faith is the opposite of depression, faith despises bitterness, and there is no room for self demands in the life of a person who professes life-changing faith! The people of God are called to walk by faith and not by what they see with their natural eye. This is the challenge: not to be preoccupied with your circumstances but to be consumed with your faith. Faith is the overcoming, conquering attitude that brazenly professes that our God is in charge. The "ites" do not determine your destiny—your faith determines your destiny! Faith is saying, with Jehosophat, "I will not be moved! I will not be shaken! Our God reigns!"

Faith is actually a response to fear because when the situation is out of my control it is in God's control. I have discovered that it really is more fun to believe! There is much more outright pleasure in living a life of unabashed faith than in allowing every waking moment to be gripped by fear.

I BELIEVE IN MIRACLES!

"Believe in Miracles!" is the bold proclamation across the basketball court of my collegiate alma mater. I have taken those three words and have built a life upon them. I do believe in miracles because I believe in the God of the miraculous. It has always been a great pleasure to me that these words were placed in the sports coliseum and not in the campus chapel. If I only believe in miracles in the sacred days of my life, what will happen on the ordinary days? It is the ordinary days that prepare us for the miraculous! It is embracing faith even when the enemies of life are tearing across your well-set boundaries that will prepare you for a miracle . . . or two . . . or three . . . or four!

God promised His people that He would be especially attentive when they took the time to stand in His house and to pray in His house. He committed to all generations that His eyes and His heart would be there perpetually! What a promise to believe in! This is a principle of faith and there is power in this principle!

Jehosophat made a confession that is still true in the twenty-first century, "No one can stand against You!" Cancer cannot stand against the Lord and neither can bankruptcy. Rebellious children, infertility, and depression are not able to stand in the presence of the King of the ages.

Jehosophat confessed his belief that the name of God was the only ruling force in the house (2 Chronicles 20:9). There is power in the house of God and there is power in the name of God! This is our birthright as Christians and it is time to stand up against the enemies in your life and be the woman of faith that you were created to be!

In the powerful prayer that Jehosophat prayed in the house of God that day, Jehosophat reminded God that when God told His people not to invade these oncoming enemies, Israel obeyed God. Jehosophat did not blame God for this invasion but he blamed the enemy. When you are fighting a battle, be very careful to whom you assign the blame. God does not send enemies into your life—they come in of their own accord and with their own force.

I hear so many Christian women whine, "I just don't understand what God is doing." Praise God that you don't understand God! If you could understand Him, you would *be* Him. Never forget that He has given you something more valuable than understanding—He has given you the peace that surpasses understanding!

I have learned from Jehosophat not to gaze upon my enemies but to set my eyes upon the Lord of Hosts! I have been taught that desperate times call for desperate measures and that there are just some occasions that call for a fast. I have learned to stay in the house of the Lord and to call upon the powerful name of the Lord. I have been taught to blame the enemy and not to blame God. I have learned not to be consumed with the "Ites" in my life but to be consumed with His presence.

Jehosophat never had the opportunity to meet Matthew of the New Testament, but he knew Matthew's God and he had Matthew's faith. "With God all things are possible" (Matthew 19:26). When you have obeyed every lesson that you have learned from Jehosophat and the enemy is still coming at you from all sides, with Jehosophat and with Matthew you confess undaunted that God is able to do all things. You shout into the heavens that nothing is too difficult for the Lord!

It was then that God spoke through Jahaziel, one of the men standing in the house of the Lord. The Bible tells us that Jahaziel was six generations removed from Asaph, one of the first worship leaders recorded in the Word of God. Do you realize what the implications of Jahaziel's family lineage teach? When you are a worshipper, you will influence your family for at least six generations to come! Teaching your children and grandchildren to be worshippers is better than leaving them millions of dollars. As women of this generation, we have filled our lives and our children's lives with an extraordinary amount of busyness. The most valuable legacy that we can leave to our children and grandchildren is a love for heartfelt, passionate worship.

YOU DO NOT OWN YOUR BATTLE

Jahaziel spoke as a prophet of God and reminded the people of Judah that they should not be afraid because the battle did not belong to them but it was the Lord's battle. These are motivating words today and we should always remind one another that there is no reason to fear! You do not own your battle—God is in charge of every battle that you face. When you take ownership of your battle, you are denying God His proper place in your life. You will only experience the victory of the Lord when you give your battle back to Him! All of your fears should bring you closer to God and you should be well aware of the fact that this battle will be won with His strength not yours. All the worrying, manipulating, and talking in the world will not bring you one step closer to being the champion over your situation.

Jahaziel had been given supernatural intelligence from heavenly sources and was able to tell the warriors of Judah exactly where to position themselves geographically the next day during the battle. He prophesied that the enemy armies would come up the ascent of Ziz and that they would station themselves at the far side of the *valley* right in front of the *wilderness* of Jeruel. Your enemies are valley dwellers who are not able to escape from the wilderness! Our God lives on the mountaintop and is not threatened by wilderness-loving enemies. Do not focus on your enemies or you will be focusing on the wilderness of life. Take your eyes off the valley and lift them to the mountaintop!

If you want to experience defiant joy, you must settle the issue of fear once and for all. Fear is a strategy of the devil to steal your joy and as long as you are having lunch with fear, you will never march forward with joy. The way that you are able to abolish fear from your life once and for all is to willfully exclaim every morning when you arise, "The Lord is with me! I am never alone!"

Say this phrase when the first inkling of worry starts knocking at the door of your heart, "The Lord is with me! I am never alone!"

Repeat this phrase at night when you lay upon your bed and fears and disillusionment begin to roll over your heart like a life-threatening tsunami, "The Lord is with me! I am never alone!"

IT'S TIME FOR SOME RUG BURN!

When was the last time that you were on your face before the Lord? When you are fighting a battle, it is a position of high-level effectiveness. I have found that being on my face before the Lord is my absolute favorite thing to do! The hours that I spend smelling my rug are the times that change my heart, motivate me, and give me a view of God that I had forgotten. I intend to enter heaven with rug burn on my nose and joy in my heart! Lay yourself down on the floor before the Lord and worship Him with your whole heart. It is in that position that God will increase your capacity for joy. You will lift yourself off the well-worn rug and find yourself saying, "Enemies?! What enemies?! I don't know what you are talking about!"

When you have set yourself to seek God . . . when you have called a fast in your life . . . when you have stood in the house of God . . . when you have cried out to God in faith . . . when you have fallen down on your face in His presence . . . what is left to do? What is the next step to victory and joy?

A VERY LOUD VOICE

You sing! You shout! You proclaim loudly your praise to the Lord God of Israel. The entire citizenship of Judah and Jerusalem in one moment of time, rose to their feet and began to praise *with a very loud voice* (2 Chronicles 20:19)! When you are at an emotional crossroads in your life, it is not a time to whisper or to mumble. When you are about to go into battle, you sing at the top of your lungs and take the roof off the house.

Do you remember the prophetic words of Jahaziel, the worship leader? "You will not need to fight in this battle" (2 Chronicles 20:17).

You do not need to fight in your battle, either. You need to start shouting and singing and dancing and allow the Lord to set ambushes for you on your behalf. The Bible says that the enemies of Judah not only were defeated but that they were routed! We are more than conquerors in Christ Jesus our Lord (Romans 8:37)! When we do things God's way and not in bondage to our own ways, He will always lead us in triumph (2 Corinthians 2:14).

All of the "ites" were destroyed completely—every last one of them. The "ites" actually began killing one another while the people of Judah stood and looked on in utter amazement with thanksgiving. What the inhabitants of Jerusalem saw with their eyes made *Saving Private Ryan* look like Mickey Mouse. (I think that I forgot to tell you that this chapter is rated "R" for violent content!)

WILL YOU EVER LEARN?

The devil near learns, does he? Perhaps a more significant question is this one, "Will you learn?" Will you learn how to fight? Or will you continue on in a lifestyle of emotional excesses and a refusal to forgive? Do you really like being depressed or are you willing to give joy a chance?

Are you beginning to understand how rich in mercy God is to those who call upon Him in truth? Are you willing to see that the only way to victory is to do things His way and not your own way? Do you realize the blessing that will come upon your life when you respond in faith and not out of emotion? God always outdoes the prayers and expectations of His people. He takes great pleasure in giving to you more than you could ask or even imagine (1 Corinthians 2:9-10)! Jehosophat and his people had prayed to be delivered from the spoil of the enemy and God not only delivered them but He enriched their lives and blessed them *with* the spoil of the enemy. Only God can do that. Only God can take a potentially fatal situation and turn it into blessing and abundance for you.

When you respond to your enemies God's way, you cannot even begin to imagine the phenomenal results. However, when you take things into your own hands and resort to gossip, bitterness, anger, blaming God, or even fear you will always settle for less than the blessing of God. You will never have the peace that passes understanding or defiant joy if you fight your battles like an old man and not like a new man.

The blessing of God was enormous on the lives of these people who had chosen to fight with worship, respond in faith, and exhibit a little bit of rug burn on their noses. They entered a time of blessing, of joy, of rest, and of peace. That is better than happily ever after, isn't it?

Chapter Six

Defying Your Emotions

Your Emotions Determine Your Destiny

Craig and our youngest son, Jordan, were flying across country one beautiful spring morning. They were returning home from a great father-son time together and were having a blast observing people, solving world problems, and challenging one another to mental puzzles. Jordan, at sixteen, was asking all of the questions that he had stored in his heart and Craig, the father of yet another teenaged boy, was taking the opportunity to share his wisdom concerning girls, career choices, girls, how to be a good driver, girls, the disciplines of life, girls . . . well, I think that you get the picture!

They had just boarded their final flight of the day when they realized that the stewardess on this flight was not a stewardess at all but a steward! Jordan had never before experienced a male flight attendant and had a hard time pushing his lower jaw up to meet his top jaw. (My thoroughly politically correct son has a hard time dealing with gender variance in career choices.) Then, just prior to take off, as the pilot's voice came over the intercom, Jordan had yet another gut-punching surprise: the pilot's voice was not that of a safe, stable, experienced male but it was the voice of an extremely young woman! Craig could not help but notice the incredulity on Jordan's face and casually mentioned to his incredulous son, "I'll bet this flight will have a lot of ups and downs."

Jordan responded in true sixteen-year-old fashion, "Yeah, and I bet that we have to stop at every bathroom between here and Pittsburgh!"

ARE YOU FROM VENUS OR MARS? OR MAYBE PLUTO?

A-H-H-H-H-H-H! The difference between men and women! Who can even begin to catalog all of the disparate ways of men and women? Surely at the top of that toxic, eternal list would be "emotions." Have you met a man yet who understands the women in his life every day of every month? Women embrace their emotions . . . men hold them at arm's length in some imaginary force field. Women actually are intimately acquainted with every little nuance of each minute feeling and can verbalize their emotions anytime, anyplace, anywhere. Men get a blank look in their eyes when you ask the simple question, "Honey, tell me how you are feeling." First of all, most men would not know a feeling if it jumped off the TV screen and landed in their glass of coke let alone, express an emotion. You might as well ask them to empty the dishwasher for you, or worse yet, spend the day after Thanksgiving together at the mall! Their resounding answer would unequivocally be, "You must be crazy!"

Why are women so defined by the acute awareness they hold concerning their emotional state? Women are meticulously mindful of the utter exhilaration of an emotional high and of the barren devastation of a tragic, theatrical valley.

Women understand that emotions can be delightful—the awe-inspiring warmth that you feel as you hold your newborn baby, or the heartfelt happiness that reaches down and embraces your entire family when gathered around the plentiful table on Thanksgiving Day.

Women are all too aware that emotions can also be ruinous—the horror you feel when you hear your husband has lost his job, or the anger that wells up inside of you every time you think of that teacher who verbally abused you.

Some emotions are surprising—the memories that flood to the surface when you receive the invitation to your high school reunion, or when you are informed in a long-distance telephone call that you are about to be a grandmother for the very first time.

Not all emotions take you on a roller coaster ride because some emotions actually serve as a stabilizing force in one's life—the strength that you feel after a comforting conversation with a mentor or a solid friend in the Lord, the quiet peace that enters your heart after spending an evening with your husband of twenty-eight years.

Emotions are also able to express your intensity—the passion of anger when you feel that someone has mistreated your child, or the indignation that you feel when someone has gossiped about a person whom you love dearly.

Emotions are able to communicate your indifference to a situation or event—yawning at your best friend's never-ending video of her trip to Turkey, ignoring the phone when caller ID tells you that it is the neighborhood gossip calling you once again!

DEFINITION AND DESTINY

Your emotions define who you are as a unique individual due to the fact that most everyone perceives you by your reactions or by your tendencies. You are emotionally fingerprinted by your tendency to overreact or over express yourself. It is hard to escape the reputation of being a moody person or the fact that you quickly show your jealousy when someone else has experienced a resounding success. If you easily become bitter when wronged, your friends and family will walk on thin ice when in your company.

Your emotional reactions to life immediately measure your level of maturity. Are you acting like a two-year-old, a teenager, or a full-grown adult? Do you give vent to childish reactions, junior high sass, or wise responses to life?

You are interpreted by your heart echoes to life and are categorized by those life currents as well. If you tear up while talking about your children, a symphony, or the wonder of creation people will instantly discern a soft, beautiful spirit.

I am a bona fide Christmas-aholic! I start playing Christmas music every year on October 1.

It's true . . . October 1 marks the first official day of Christmas for my clan and it is nearly categorized as a national holiday by all who know us. I call the children who live far away at 6:00 AM and play the McLeod family theme song over my wireless connection, "I'll Be Home for Christmas!" We have two Christmas trees adorning our home and garlands around every single downstairs window. Pine-scented candles burn for nearly two months prior to the season of holly and mistletoe and Christmas movies are viewed nearly every night for three festive months. I am known and defined by my love for the most wonderful time of the year.

Not only do your emotions define who you are as an individual but your emotions also have the capacity to create your very destiny. If your emotions are out of control, so will be your marriage, your parenting skills, and your relationships at work or in your family. If your emotions are unmanageable and wild, you will be destined for failure in every single area of your life. Your children will be afraid of you, your husband will resent you, you will have no true friends, and you will lose many jobs. Your emotions are creating your future in nearly every possible way.

If, however, you are a woman of quiet strength, who shows kindness in the face of gossip and is patient when wronged then you will have too many friends to count and you will receive promotions and bonuses from now until 2057! If you have your angry outbursts under control and would not nag your husband if someone actually paid you to nag, then your marriage will be one continual honeymoon and your children will rise up and call you blessed.

JUST ANSWER ONE QUESTION FOR ME

If you know that your emotions give your life definition and that your emotions also create your destiny, then why in the world have you allowed your emotions to rage out of control? Your life is not an amusement park and you should not be giving hourly thrill rides on an out of control, colossal roller coaster.

Why do you lose your temper when your two-year-old acts, thinks, and talks just like a two-year-old?

Why do you worry when your teenager is fifteen minutes late or when you receive an unexpected bill in the mail?

Why does a bad headache automatically turn into a brain tumor in your mind?

Why do you spew anger upon your husband—the man of your dreams, your former prince in shining armor—when he comes home with yet another speeding ticket for driving too fast?

Why do you get frustrated with your family and speak impatiently to them just minutes before the pastor and his wife walk into the door? You will be sweet and kind to the man of God but with one angry look you can cause your teenage daughter's blood to curdle.

Why does Christmas—the season of the birthday of our King—cause you to worry about finances, give vent to weariness, and complain about busyness?

Why do you feel constrained to communicate every feeling and emotion that is simmering in your heart when you do not get your own way?

Why indeed?

I'LL ANSWER ONE QUESTION FOR YOU!

You are not going to like my answer . . . I hope that you are sitting down as you read this . . . take a deep breath . . . get ready to deal with your anger at me . . . (It's too late to take the book back!)

The reason that our emotions are out of control is because we love our feelings more than we love Him. *We would rather have it our way than have it His way and we are more consumed with self-ishness than with selflessness.* Our emotions have gone haywire because we like to believe that we are in control and that He is not. We think that we are the only ones that could possibly be right and that the world is certainly wrong. (And that definitely includes my husband AND my mother-in-law!)

Sadly, we have agreed with our culture in the commitment to making sure that life is solidly built around the Great Number One! We have decidedly chosen to forget that the virtue of self-control is a character trait of priceless value. Self-control is a difficult character trait to embrace while living in a culture of Miss Piggy, enormous credit card debt, and "It's All About Me!" Trying to progress from "out of control" to "self-control" is a mighty hard issue. It's like trying to dig a staple from underneath your fingernail. It hurts . . . you have to remove it . . . but it is utter torture while it is happening!

CONTROL ME! CONTROL ME!

Matthew and Christopher were such adorable little boys; their hair was always combed to perfec-tion, their rooms were always straightened, they had little halos shining over their cherubic heads, they never spoke an unkind word to one another. . . .

Well, they were adorable! At least to me, but I was keenly aware of the fact that they were normal, rough and tumble preschoolers who needed my constant supervision. Matthew, who is two years older than Christopher, was built like a miniature football player—he was sturdy and stocky and wore a size 6x while still too young for kindergarten. Christopher, on the other hand, has always had the world's greatest metabolism. At barely three-years-old, he was wiry and lively and had a grand time jumping from the couch to the coffee table and back again. Christopher, the younger, loved to pummel Matthew, the elder, even though Matthew could have flattened Christopher with one swoop of his defensive-linebacker body. Whenever Christopher would start pounding his older brother, Matthew would not fight back but would start crying for help from "*Mama!*"

One long winter's evening in Buffalo, Craig had enough of our miniature David beating up his older brother, Goliath, and told me that he was going to teach Matthew how to fight back.

"Oh, no, you won't! You will not teach my darling little boys that revenge is the answer," I exclaimed in a manner that could have won me the Nobel Peace Prize. "You will have to come up with a different strategy."

Craig went dutifully into the living room and began to teach Matthew that when Christopher started to beat up on him, Matthew could just take Christopher's little arms and hold them at his sides and control him.

"You are bigger than he is. You can just hold his arms down at his sides and control Christopher." Craig said to our future all-state football player.

The next morning, after Craig had left for the office, I was in the kitchen making the boys a winter lunch of grilled cheese sandwiches and red jello while the boys were in the living room watching *Mr. Rogers' Neighborhood*. All of a sudden, I heard it start again. I heard Christopher jump from the couch to the coffee table and onto his prodigious older brother. Christopher started to pummel Matthew and Matthew started to yell for *"Mama!"* Before I could reach the living room, which was all of ten steps away, I could hear Christopher encouragingly yell, "Control me, brother! Control me!"

It is time—it is past time—to get your emotions under God's control. It is time to call an end to gossip, bitterness, the silent treatment, and the tendency to spew out in anger against those you love the very most. Maybe it is time for you to cry out, "Control me, God! Control me!"

CANCEL THE PARTY!

One of the underlying factors in our addiction to allowing our emotions to spiral out of control is the self-pity factor. You feel sorry for yourself so you gossip and assassinate someone else's character which you think will somehow make you look smarter, better, or happier. You feel sorry for yourself and hate your lot in life so you nag your husband or berate your three-year-old. Your life did not turn out the way that you thought that it would so you are impatient with your daughter-in-law or do not put in a full day's work. It is entirely possible that low self-esteem is the birthing room of self-pity. You do not like yourself and you hate your life so you shoot yourself in your emotional foot and exhibit the symptoms of anger, jealousy, or worry.

Some psychological experts contend that emotions such as jealousy, anger, or impatience are just part of the human nature. That might be true—but remember that you are endowed with a superhuman nature! You have the mind of Christ and the power of the Holy Spirit, which empower you to conquer the base aspects of our humanity. It's time to end your pity party before another day of your life goes by.

THE MATHEMATICS OF EMOTIONAL STABILITY

We have already seen that emotions are not all bad but it is of utmost importance that you sift through your emotions and decide which are good and which are bad. It is imperative that you examine your emotional tendencies and embrace the positive while sweeping away the negative.

Being in love with your husband is a good thing but the sheer exhilaration of romance will not always last. Love is a choice and you must build your marriage upon conviction not on roses and diamond rings.

I have had to learn that becoming excited about the holidays is a wonderful part of my personality but I have to be very careful not to overextend myself in the areas of scheduling, spending, and eating!

The very best endowment that a mother can give to her children is unconditional, expressive love. But, mothers, it is not a good thing to brag about your children, to expect them to be perfect, or to build your life around their activities.

Enjoying your job and using your gifts, talents, and abilities is true pleasure in life but using your profession as a barometer for your self-esteem is a sign of weakness not of strength. Neglecting your family, your church, and your health because your work consumes your life is nothing short of addiction.

An extremely important tenet of Christianity is to live your life by the motto, "He must increase and I must decrease" (John 3:30). I can guarantee you that the pure joy of heaven will come pouring down into your home, your heart, and your life when you pray this prayer every day of your life:

"Lord, I pray that today there will be much less of me and much more of You in my life. I like Who You are so much more than I like who I am. I pray that I will focus less on my feelings and more on my faith in You. I pray for a lessening of my out of control emotions and for more of Your involvement in the issues of my heart. Father God, decrease my tantrums and increase Your stability. In Jesus' powerful name I pray. Amen."

KILL THE BEAST

It is of vital importance to identify the specific emotions with which you deal, rather than dealing with generalizations, which only help you to sweep emotional instability under the rug. With what one emotion do you truly struggle? Perhaps, like me, you struggle with two or three or four out of control emotions. The challenge is to allow Him to increase in my life in these specific areas so that my emotions do not spiral out of control.

It always comes back to the Word of God, doesn't it? It always is about spending time in His presence in prayer and praise and in the wonder of worship. It comes to polishing up the full armor that He has so generously given to us for our protection. It always comes back to dying to self.

The lives that the men and women of faith in the New Testament were called to lead are nothing short of incredible. On a daily basis, they were faced with imprisonment and with the tortures of the Roman government; they were separated from family and friends and were forced to watch those that they loved the most be stoned to death. They suffered shipwreck, starvation, homelessness, and numerous other types of life-threatening peril. As I meditate on their struggle with persecution, I am reminded of my struggle with wild and tormenting emotions.

There was a time in my life when I struggled with the haunting ghosts of emotional instability on a daily and even an hourly basis. Mothers of young children and teenagers, you are fully aware that some hours are good and some are akin to having your toenails pulled out one at a time. Single women realize that some days are a walk in the park while other days the beasts of loneliness are howling outside your bedroom door. Every morning when I wake up, I have learned to choose death: death to self and death to preferences; I choose death to my out of control emotions. I choose to say, "I will not be angry with my children today and I will not be frustrated with my schedule. I will love the little lady on the other end of the phone who calls me every single day. I will not gossip and I will not be negative." You see, I have learned what my issues are and I commit them to prayer before my feet hit the floor in the morning.

Emotions can be like wild beasts in your life . . . just go ahead and admit it! If once a month is a gargoyle, then menopause might as well be Tyrannosaurus rex. There is no hope for you unless you kill the beast! Kill the wild beast known as your emotional state and die to self! When you truly die to self, there is more room for Christ to live in your heart.

The bad company of emotions gone wild will kill any remnant of goodness in you. Any good that you accomplish will be rendered useless if you remain controlled by the beast.

It is a painful lesson to learn, but we must convince ourselves that our emotions do not tell the truth to us . . . our emotions are liars through and through. What drives you to distraction today—you will certainly laugh at tomorrow. What you cannot live without today—tomorrow will only be a haunting melody. Once you believe the fact that your emotions are deceptive, it is time to become sober minded. Life is not all about you, your preferences, how comfortable you are, or even making your dreams come true. It's not! It is just not!

The more you know God, the more you pray for Him to increase in your life and for you to decrease, you will stop the emotional sin state in which you have been stranded and you will miraculously and suddenly be in control of your emotions. A fresh breeze of freedom will blow through your life and the chains of bondage will miraculously drop from your heart. You have the power, by virtue of your emotions, to literally usher God's presence into your world. When you are a woman of peace, your home will be a place of peace. When joy has washed away the last vestige of depression, your marriage will take on new radiance. When you have embraced hope in its fullest measure, your friends will come to you for encouragement and advice. He must increase and I must decrease!

WHEN ARE YOU THE WEAKEST?

It is important to recognize the difference between your soul and your spirit when dealing with emotions. The spirit is higher than the soul in terms of eternal value. The spirit is the life principle bestowed upon man by God whereas the soul is the seat of personality. The soul encompasses the sentiment by which man perceives, reflects, feels, and desires. The soul is the birthplace of one's emotional response to life. When the Bible references your soul, it is an exacting definition of that which is the springboard for your attitudes, tendencies, and personality.

King David was well acquainted with his soulish responses to life and often spoke of the battle between his soul and his spirit. He knew that his soul had longings that even changed from time to time. Like King David, it is important for you to identify that for which your soul longs. For what does your soul long? Does your soul long to get even with someone who has wronged you? Does your soul long to have its own way in every situation? Perhaps your soul just longs to ventilate and spew everything that it conjures up. You will never solve this issue with out of control emotions until your soul yearns for the things of God. Your emotions will always be out of balance until your soul's one desire in life is to embrace His will and not your own. You will never be the beneficiary of defiant joy until you are able to confidently proclaim, "My life is not about me and about what I want. My life will no longer be centered upon my desires and my feelings. My soul's deepest desires will only be satisfied by time spent in His presence" (Psalm 84:1).

I have purposed, in my life, that no longer will my heart whine, murmur, or complain but instead my heart will sing one, uninterrupted song and it will be a melody that resounds of sterling joy! Next time that you feel as though you are about to explode in anger, sing for joy! When you are tempted to criticize or gossip, why don't you try singing for joy instead? When you feel the snowflakes of impatience threaten to become an avalanche of anger take a deep breath, don't count to ten, just sing for joy!

In order to deal with your emotions effectively, it is imperative that you reprogram yourself and plan ahead. Retrain your base instinctive reaction to a spiritual response of joy. When your three-year-old has had yet another "accident," sing a song with your children instead of yelling. (Don't you just love potty training?!) When your mother-in-law critiques your cooking even though you have been married to your husband longer than he lived at home, start singing, *Great Is Your Faithfulness* instead of giving into resentment. When your husband hurts your feelings at just the wrong time of the month, break out into *his* favorite praise and worship song. When

Valentine's Day is just around the corner and you are alone yet another year, do not give in and croon, *I'm So Lonely Without You*! but belt out a heartfelt chorus of *You Are All I Want—You Are All I Ever Needed*! Sing it like you mean it to the Man Who loves you just the way you are.

You must plan ahead in this whitewashing of your soul and this means that you need to know exactly when you are the weakest.

If you know that your boss is going to threaten to fire everyone around April 15, plan ahead. You can think of creative ways to encourage him and the staff around you. The reason that you work at your place of employment is NOT to earn a paycheck, but it is to bring the presence of Jesus Christ into that place.

If you know that the date of your anniversary is a hard time for you because of your husband's untimely death, go on a vacation with some friends or take your children out to dinner that night. You must not sit home alone and longingly look at your wedding album while playing "your song" on the CD player. You must know when you are the weakest and plan ahead.

There are many practical ideas that you can employ in order to handle your emotions in a healthy manner and to help yourself divert from the stress of the moment. Instead of flying off the handle at your neighbor whose dog leaves little remnants in your yard, you might choose to go for a jog or clean that closet that has threatened to explode for the past decade.

If you need counseling, do not put it off. Many Christian women find great strength in talking to a counselor who will help them with their out of control emotional responses to life. Or, perhaps engaging yourself in an activity that you enjoy such as working in the yard or reading a great book might help as an emotional distraction. You might choose to count to ten . . . or one hundred . . . or one million. For one of my best friends, the thing that always works is getting in the shower, turning it on hot and full blast, and then screaming! (The name will not be revealed to protect the innocent!) When the children were little and I was overwhelmed with crayons on the wall, apple juice on the couch, and never a moment of free time, I would go to the grocery store late at night and just walk up and down the aisles while looking for an adult with whom to converse!

These practical things are all very beneficial and I recommend them highly, however, please remember that these practical things will only help you for that one time. Then, the next time you hit a weak moment, you will have to make a practical choice all over again. These practical suggestions merely put a band-aid on the gaping wound that your extreme emotional reactions have caused in your ability to relate to others.

If you would like the antidote rather than the band-aid, the cure is more of Him and less of me. The cure is singing for joy and staying in the Word of God. The cure is developing an effective, fervent prayer life that does not focus on you but on the needs of others. The cure is choosing to live like a mature Christian who exhibits the character of Christ in every situation.

MAKING YOURSELF AT
HOME IN HIS PRESENCE

How blessed are those who dwell in your house! They are ever praising you. How blessed is the man whose strength is in You, in whose heart are the highways to Zion! Passing through the valley of weeping they make it a place of springs. The early rain also covers it with blessings. They go from strength to strength and everyone of them appears before God in Zion.

Psalm 84: 4-7

There will be a heavenly blessing on your life when you allow Him to be your strength and you choose not to turn to your emotions in the time of crisis. If you desire to be a woman of strength and if you desire to master your emotions and not allow them to master you, this is how you will do life: You will make yourself at home in His presence! You will read your Bible every day because you *want* to not because you *have* to. (Reading for enjoyment <u>does</u> include the Bible, you know!) You will listen to praise and worship music every chance you have on every single day of the year. You will flatten yourself before him and experience rug burn on the tip of your nose. You will take your shoes off, settle back, and enjoy the gift of His presence!

Making yourself at home in His presence may present a great challenge for you and you may not look forward to the struggle that is going to ensue while you try to practice His presence. I have felt this way in my life too many times to count and I found it imperative to convince myself that I was sure to be a better mother, a more loving wife, and a more wonderful person if I enveloped this discipline as a pleasure and not as a nuisance.

When an athlete prepares for a marathon, he or she sets aside hours every day to exercise, to eat right, and to run mile after mile after mile. Many marathon participants must set aside five to seven hours a day in preparation for this monumental event in their life. You are preparing for a marathon as well, it is called the marathon of life. Your marathon may include the mountains of motherhood or going down into the valley of sickness or poverty. You may encounter singleness, a difficult marriage, or infertility on the path that you traverse. I am determined to cross my finish line with the word "JOY!" stamped in blazing colors across my chest! You only are given one chance to do life and to do it well—this is your moment to embrace His character and be filled with His joy.

I proactively schedule hours every week for prayer, personal worship, fasting, listening to His voice, and for reading my Bible. I lay aside other things such as television, the computer, magazines, or books that do not enhance my relationship with Him. You might not agree with some of the choices that I make but they have been necessary in my quest to increase my capacity for joy. I rarely go out for lunch with friends or commit myself to committees because I know that if I do those things, my time in His presence will be curtailed. I simply cannot afford less of Him.

I have also learned to fast from the fun stuff of life until I truly am at home in His presence. I want to be more at home in His presence than I am in my emotions. I remind myself every day that my emotions define who I am as a person and they also determine my destiny.

A PRICELESS TREASURE

In 1979, Craig and I moved to Mobile, Alabama to serve on the staff of a growing church. Our first Friday evening in that azalea hewn city, we were invited to the warm home of Carolyn and Bernard Hogan for a five-star dinner. She served homemade lasagna, an exotic salad, Italian bread piping hot from the oven, and for dessert we had brownies "with the crust cut off." (I always thought the crust of anything was the best part!) Her impact on my life has long outlasted the remembrance of a delicious meal served with southern hospitality. Carolyn became my mentor and friend on that very evening. She is ten years older than I and so has experienced all of life about ten years before I have. When her children were in the late elementary and early teen years, I was only starting to have babies. When my children were involved in Little League baseball and piano recitals, her children were going away to college. When my children were presenting me with the challenges of adolescence, she was experiencing the joy of becoming a grandmother. Carolyn has been my mentor both spiritually and emotionally. Carolyn loves me enough to correct me and encourage me. She will not allow me to settle for being less than my very best. I can tell her anything and I know that she will not patronize my emotions but will call me higher in the Lord. Being Carolyn Hogan's friend has been a priceless treasure in an otherwise fairly ordinary life.

All Christian women need to find their "Carolyn Hogan." Whether you are eighteen or eighty-two, God has someone chosen especially for you who will love you enough to correct you and will allow you to be nothing less than your very best self. If, you have been a Christian longer than five years, you need to *be* a Carolyn Hogan to a woman younger in the Lord who needs an accountant or a mentor. I can guarantee you that this relationship will be a priceless treasure in your life as well!

A PUMPKIN MUFFIN AND A FLASHLIGHT

Right now, I want you to feel as if we are sitting across the breakfast table from one another sharing our second cup of coffee and a warm pumpkin muffin. (Well, maybe not warm because I can guarantee you that I didn't make it . . . I bought it yesterday at my favorite bakery anticipating your arrival!) If we were sitting across the table from one another and you were pouring out your heart with me concerning your emotional instability, I would have to share this Scripture with you. We would stay at the table together until you had memorized it because I know that this Scripture has the potential to change your life: "Search me, O God, and know my heart; Try me and know my anxious thoughts; And see if there be any hurtful way in me, and lead me in the everlasting way" (Psalm 139: 23-24).

After we had memorized these familiar verses together, then we would pray together. I would ask

God to search you and to reveal your emotional weaknesses in all areas of your life. I know that sometimes I can be so blinded and deeply in bondage to my feelings that I cannot be a good judge of what is going on in my heart—only God can do that. After we closed our prayer with a heartfelt "amen" and a box full of tissues, then we would rummage around in one of my drawers for a pen that actually worked and a scrap of paper. I would ask you at that point to write down what God had shown you concerning your emotional weaknesses. After you pray, expect God to talk! Do not "blow off" what He shows you, or think to yourself, "Oh! That certainly can't be God!" Oh yes it can be God and it probably is!

After praying for God to reveal your emotional weaknesses and asking Him to be the judge of what is transpiring in your heart, if the first thing that comes to your mind is the tendency to nag your husband or berate your children, then that is God shining His heavenly flashlight into places of darkness in your life. Suddenly you may recall being rude to the woman at work who talks too much or blowing your horn at the senior citizen who drives too slowly—God is lighting up some dark passages in the roadways of your heart.

God may warn you of the deep issues of your soul that only He knows about or the intricacies of your heart. He is the Great Observer of people, you know, and He has spent *your* entire life observing how you are living your life. God may show you that you have an anger problem during a certain time of the month. *Deal with it!* He may reveal that you are at your emotional worst on the day that you sit down to pay the bills. *Deal with it!* God may delicately point out the fact that you are too sensitive and you rehearse the times that a certain person has hurt your feelings. *Deal with it!* God has shown me that when I allow my calendar to become too crowded and when I am too busy that I am not a very nice person to live with! I have two choices—cut down on the busyness or choose to be a nicer person no matter what time I got up this morning. You see, I too, have to *deal with it!*

A LEGACY THAT WILL LAST A LIFETIME

Can we linger for just a minute longer over a third cup of coffee? I know that we both probably have things to do and people to see, but I would just love to share with you one more Scripture that has enabled me to dig myself out of the mountainous manure of my emotions. Let this Scripture simmer on the back burner of your soul. "Oh! That they had such a heart in them! That they would trust Me and keep all My commandments always, that it may be well with them and with their sons forever!" (Deuteronomy 5:29).

This is a divine promise that has the capability of bringing closure to your issues concerning your emotional addictions. Do you have a heart to keep all of His commandments and to trust Him in all seasons of your life? If you do, there is a promise that is yours in its fullest measure: it will be well with you and with your children forever! Instead of passing down a legacy of anger and bitterness, you have the potential to leave to your children a treasure of joy and peace!

THE LAND OF IDOLATRY

Our culture, in tandem with pop psychology, has made our emotions into well-polished idols. We have been taught, "If it feels good, then do it!"

"Express yourself! There is no wrong way to feel," our culture has convinced us.

"It's all about me," has been the mantra of ad agencies, clothing companies, fast-food restaurants, and child psychologists for too many years to count.

"Allow your children to express themselves," child experts have unwisely taught, although they have never had children themselves. No wonder we are known as the "I Feel!" generation.

Feelings have become more important than convictions and emotions have usurped the traditional prominence of the Word of God. Emotional preferences have eclipsed the difference between right and wrong as well as between good and bad. When you enter the maze of gargantuan feelings or of a soulish response to an issue, you are entering the land of idolatry.

It is nearly impossible to exit this maze and soon your rationalizations will become the poison of self-inflicted mortality. "I get to yell because I am the mom and they are the kids!"

Where did that come from? *You get to yell* because you have been granted the God-given privilege of raising your children to be men and women of God who exhibit the fruits of the spirit? *You get to yell?* I don't think so.

"*I get to spend* money because my husband is a workaholic who doesn't pay any attention to me and the children." *You get to spend* so that you can feel better about your husband's shortcomings? I don't think so.

"I get to talk about the church because I am, quite frankly, more spiritual than even the pastor. I know more than he does!" *You get to talk about the church* because you think you are better than someone or something? I don't think so.

When your thought processes turn in this dark direction, you are living in the land of emotional idolatry and suddenly, your emotions have become more important than your relationship with God. If you give in to your emotions in even one area, the idolatry will grow exponentially and you will be in the forest of no return. You might need to ask God if you have allowed your emotions to become a brightly shining idol in your life or a security blanket that you cannot live without.

If you feel that you have been allowing your emotions to become your idols there is one way out of this maze: repentance. You may need to repent to your husband or call a family meeting and repent to your children, both those who are grown and those who are still at home. You may need to repent to friends, to coworkers, or to your parents. God may be calling you to repent to your pastor or the spiritual leadership at church because you have allowed a negative spirit to infest your ability to pray for them.

Repentance is guaranteed to set you free and to deliver you from the swamp of emotion-based living. Repentance is the only path out of the emotional maze that you have created for your life. Your emotions define you as a person and they have the power of creating your destiny. Your emotions have the capability of ushering the presence of God into your world. This will only happen if you are committed to the mathematic formula of a healthy emotional life: He must increase and I must decrease.

Chapter Seven

An Eight-Step Program to Sure and Certain Joy!

How to Access the Character of God in Your Life!

"Mary Houston" . . . what a plain name. No pizzazz, no pretense about a name like that, just vanilla, plain old, "Mary Houston." Mary lived in a nondescript home that was more than a bit run-down. It was a house well beyond its prime and to a realtor just might be described as a "handyman's special." Her well-lived in home was on a street in a town that has never been written about in a history book.

Mary was known as the best cook in town and loved sharing her culinary "homecookin'" with anyone who was in need. She cared for the pets of vacationing neighbors and wrote poetry for every occasion. Mary loved making crafts of all different shapes and sizes. Since she had no children of her own, preceding every holiday, she would always invite a whole passel of neighborhood kids into her living room so that they could make crafts together. I learned how to weave pot holders in her living room and that you could color macaroni a variety of colors! Who knew?!

Mary visited widows, new comers to town, and mothers of nursing babies. She would pick up your mail for you and buy your groceries, all on the same rainy day. Mary knew what you were likely to buy at the corner grocery store and so would sort her coupons in piles according to family preference. At least once a month, we found a packet of coupons between our screen door and the winter door.

Mary would bring flowers from her garden to grace your dinner table for no particular occasion. She canned her vegetables and gave them away, baked homemade bread and gave it away, and once she had completed reading a magazine or book it would find its way into someone else's home.

I never heard one critical word out of her mouth—I guess that's why I always felt so safe around her. I knew that if she didn't talk unkindly about others, she probably wouldn't talk about me, either. Although I am now four decades removed from childhood, I can still hear the tinkle of her laughter as she walked from door to door just stopping by to bless people, recite a piece of poetry, or share a favorite song. The joy that sparkled out of her inner being touches me to this very day. As a child, I did not define it as joy, I just knew that I liked what she had and when I grew up, I wanted to be just like her!

Oh! I think that I have forgotten to tell you something about Mary . . . Did I tell you that Mary was crippled? Her legs had been paralyzed from the waist down since childhood due to a devastating case of polio. But, crippled legs could never stop a woman of her emotional tenor. I can still see her today making her way up and down the streets of my hometown, holding on to her walker as she dragged the bottom half of her body from house to house.

Mary Houston was well acquainted with her Father and with the character of His legacy. Mary may have been the most beautiful woman that I have ever had the pleasure of knowing, perhaps she is the most significant woman that I have ever known. She is certainly the kindest woman that I have ever known. I believe that kindness and joy are Siamese twins in life—you really cannot have one without the other. A kind person has found a reason to sing and a joyful person is a giver not a taker.

START ACTING LIKE YOUR DAD

God is rich—He is the richest man alive but His wealth is not measured in the number of zeros behind a number. His richness is not judged in real estate holdings, although He does own the entire world. His wealth is not determined by the jewels in His cases, although He does make the Queen of England look like poor, white trash. The wealth of your Heavenly Father is measured in His vast kindness toward us who are His children! If your wealth were measured by the amount of kindness that you exhibit to others, which is heaven's standard of economic success, how rich would you be? Would you be in the bracket of Donald Trump? Or perhaps you would more closely resemble the character of Ebeneezer Scrooge?

Do you remember when you were a child and the other children on the playground would find great pleasure concerning the bragging rights of their father's strength?

"My dad's bigger than your dad!"

"Oh, yeah! Well, my dad's stronger than your dad!"

"My dad can beat your dad up!"

How about this one . . . "My Dad is kinder than anyone in all of recorded history!"

The only kindness that we are able to demonstrate comes from our heavenly genetics. He has more kindness than Mother Theresa, Oprah Winfrey, and the American Red Cross combined! His kindness surpasses anything known to mankind and exceeds the ability to comprehend. His kindness is called "loving kindness." There is an eternal display of show-and-tell in progress and we just happen to be the show-and-tell of His kindness!

Not only is His kindness on display through our lives but every single thing in us that has any redemptive quality at all, is because of Him. Every bit of goodness in us is only a reflection of His goodness and any mercy that we are able to exhibit is because His character is at work within us.

A PRECIOUS PROMISE

I love to study the Bible, do you? I can certainly assure you that if there is any joy in my soul at all, and if there are any healthy emotional boundaries that I embrace, it is because I have fallen passionately and hopelessly in love with the Word of God. I hope that you, too, enjoy studying the Bible, because that is what we are about to do together! I am about to take you on a fantastic journey through the Word of God that will literally wipe out all leftover fragments of depression in your heart. This section of the Bible is going to take you beyond depression and into the destiny that God has ordained for you. Are you ready? Go and get your Bible, a notebook, and find a pen or pencil. (If you find a pen that works, could you bring one for me as well? Thanks . . . I knew that I could count on you!)

"Grace and peace be multiplied to you in the knowledge of God and of Jesus our Lord," are the Words of life that are found in 2 Peter 1:2. Did you realize that God does not want to give you just a smidgen of grace and just a tad of peace? He wants your portion of grace and peace to be multiplied as you get to know God and Jesus on a more intimate level. The more time that you spend in the Bible and in lingering at His throne, you will discover that you will be more gracious to people! (That means you will be kinder and less critical.) You will also be aware of the fact that your tendencies to worry, criticize, or stress-out will fade away in the distance because you will be a woman whose peace has exponential qualities! If you want your grace and peace to be multiplied it will only happen as you become better acquainted with Him and as you increase in the knowledge of all that He is and all that He does.

"Seeing that His divine power has granted to us everything pertaining to life and godliness, through the true knowledge of Him who called us by His own glory and excellence" (2 Peter 1:3). I like that! Your Father loves you so much that He has already provided everything that you need that pertains to life and godliness. WOW! What an exciting possibility! This verb, *has granted*, is in the perfect tense which means that it is as

done as it is ever going to be! He gave it all at once. The question is, did you receive it? He gave you the whole package in one fell swoop—you have everything that you need to live a godly life while here on earth! What a truly miraculous probability! I get to live just the way He would if He were here on earth. When you have Jesus Christ, you have absolutely everything that you need to deal with the inconsistencies of a mortal-bound life. You have been given, by His divine power, everything you need to deal with PMS, depression, a critical spirit, a low-income level, infertility, a cranky husband, *no* husband . . . and the list goes on and on and on. How do you get everything that you need? Once again, this verse tells us that we receive it *through the true knowledge of Him.* Do you know Him? Do you really know Him? Do you know Him intimately? How many verses of the Bible have you memorized this year? You must memorize Scripture if you want to know Him! Have you listened to Him lately? Or do you just do all the talking when you are together? If you will read your Bible, memorize the Word of God, and then listen for His voice, it is certain that you will, through His power, have everything that you need to live a life of extravagant joy.

THE REAL DEAL

"For by these He has granted to us His precious and magnificent promises, so that by them you may become partakers of the divine nature, having escaped the corruption that is in the world by lust" (2 Peter 1:4). It is a precious promise that we are able to become actual partakers of the divine

nature of God Himself. We are not an earthly counterfeit of a heavenly being . . . we are the real deal of heaven on earth! We are empowered to look, talk, walk, act, and emote just like Jesus did! We have the potential, while on earth, to live by the very power of God (2 Corinthians 5:17).

God's power can actually replace our weaknesses in absolutely all areas of our life. This promise, full of hope and potentiality, guarantees that we do not have to be corrupted by the lusts of this world. We do not have to be dragged down by keeping up with the Trumps or by being a political power broker at work or by dressing to entice. When we walk and live in the Spirit of God, we are walking in the opposite direction of our natural tendencies. We are called above our human bent and beyond our genetic predisposition. The highest calling of my life is not to a six-figure income or publishing a best seller or being a sought after worship leader, but it is the calling that when we have chosen to walk by the Spirit of the living God, we will no longer carry out all those putrid desires of the flesh (Galatians 5:16).

EMOTIONAL ELBOW GREASE

This calling to dodge the lusts of the flesh and to no longer carry out the desires of the flesh is not some ethereal impossibility but the Word of God offers an extremely practical application to this challenge. Peter, in these verses from 2 Peter, presents an eight-step program that will guarantee you a way out of the dredge of your emotional overdrive. *"Now, for this very reason also, applying all diligence and in your faith supply moral excellence and in your moral excellence, knowledge"* (2 Peter 1:5).

What is the reason that Peter is presenting the eight-step program? It is so that you will escape the corruption that is in the world by lust and so that you will be a partaker of His divine nature. Sign me up! I will be a part of any program that enables me to be more like Jesus and less like me.

Before Peter introduces the first step in this overcoming, conquering program, he warns us that it is going to be hard work. We must be ready to work diligently to achieve His likeness while here on earth. This is going to require hard work every day of your life and you will have to apply emotional elbow grease that you never knew existed. You must be determined that you will never give up as you conquer the mountain of rugged emotions that go on as far as your heart can feel.

Working in my father's garden, when I was a child, was always a dreaded activity. As soon as the sun started to shine after a frigid western New York winter, my father could be found working up the hard soil in our family garden. Once he had completed the task of making the soil pliable enough to work with, then it was our turn. All three of his offspring could be found out in the springtime air, picking up rocks, raking leaves out of the dirt, and hoeing the garden in general. By the time the sun had set, my muscles were aching from child labor! I could barely lift my arm from the dinner table to fork the food into my tired mouth. My legs ached from top to bottom and climbing the stairs to bed was more of a torture than a relief. We were diligent workers in that one acre plot of land that in just a few months would yield a harvest of mouth-watering fruits and vegetables! Sometimes it just pays to be diligent—to work so hard that your muscles ache and you long for a well-deserved respite.

This is the kind of diligence that Paul is referring to—a diligence that might cause you to groan in pain or dread the next day but that will yield an abundant crop of godly characteristics in your life.

BECOMING A GOD-PLEASER

The first step that you must embrace is a vibrant and living faith! You must place all of your faith and trust in the belief that God is a good God in every situation of your life. Remind yourself on a daily basis that God is on your side and that He is in control of the infinite number of details in your life. I am constantly aware that without faith, it is impossible to please God (Hebrews 11:6). When I am tempted to murmur or complain or panic emotionally, I turn myself to faith and to the assurance that He has plans of a future and a hope for me (Jeremiah 29:11).

ABOVE AND NOT BELOW

Step two in this life-changing program is that we must be women of moral excellence. The world will call you to moral compromise but the Word calls you to moral excellence. It is not "just fine" to cheat on your taxes or on your husband. There is power in the words that come out of your mouth and you must make a vow never to curse or use profanity.

I refuse to gossip—I just refuse to do it. There is a woman in my life who just loves to talk about people. Ninety percent of every conversation that she initiates with me is focused on her insight into other people's lives. As she rattles away, totally unaware of my lack of participation in her soliloquy, I will gently insert the question, "So, have you read any good books lately?" There will be silence on the other end of the phone for maybe seven seconds, and then she takes right off again, slicing and dicing people who were made in the image of God, chewing them up, and then spitting them back out. When she finally comes up for air, I will nonchalantly interject, "What are you having for dinner tonight?" After a few months of this repetitive conversation, she finally said to me, "You really are not interested in what I have to say about people, are you?" To which I gently replied, "I am very interested in you but I am just not interested in talking about people."

You are a woman of moral excellence not of moral compromise. Because you live above and not below the moral quagmire of the day, you must carefully choose what television programs you watch, what movies you attend, and what books you allow yourself to read. This is no small issue in the life of a Christian woman as she fights to win back the joy that the world has counterfeited. If you are immersed in romance novels, your mind will be filled with fantasy and compromising situations. If you watch television shows in which women dress inappropriately, talk inappropriately, and leave a path of moral desolation in their wake, how will you ever drag your emotions out of the gutter?

Mike, who had just turned fifteen, came to his father one afternoon and asked permission to go with all of his friends to see a movie that had just been released. This movie had received great reviews and seemed to be on its way to winning several Academy Awards. The father, who was not born yesterday, had fully investigated the movie and knew that it visually depicted several compromising situations. The movie was not rated "G" for generally good or even "PG" for pretty good some of the time. The movie was nowhere near the "PG-13" rating which means pretty good except for the 13 times when profanity is used. The movie that Mike and his friends wanted to go see was rated "R" for rotten through and through.

As Mike fought the losing battle with his father, his parting words were, "But Dad! It doesn't have a lot of bad stuff in it! It just has a little bit and I will ignore the little bit of bad stuff, I promise."

"Mike, you need to go to your room and re-evaluate your desire to see this movie. You know that our family has a set standard and we do not under any conditions watch R-rated movies," Mike's father said quietly and kindly.

About an hour later, Mike's father went upstairs to see how his son was faring and had decided to treat him to his favorite snack—warm brownies just out of the oven. Mike slowly opened his bedroom door with a sullen look on his adolescent face.

"I love you so much, Mike that I decided to bake your favorite treat as a peace offering," the dad lovingly said.

"Thanks, Dad! You are the best!" exclaimed Mike with his face lighting up like sunshine on a summer's day.

"Oh . . . and Mike . . . I just put a little bit of the dog's poop in the batter. There really isn't much poop in there. I am sure that you will just ignore that part."

We have convinced ourselves that a little bit of compromise is not compromise at all. We have rationalized our lukewarm acceptance that it really does not matter if we dress like the world. Ladies, let me encourage you to dress like women of God not like women of the world. When you show cleavage or other parts of your body that should be covered, Satan laughs at your foolishness. His goal is to entice you to dress immodestly and then convince yourself that "everybody is doing it!" I believe that there is a way to dress in a stylish manner without being seductive. Your wardrobe can boast of class and femininity without being foolish. Wise up, ladies! Add to your faith moral excellence.

WHAT WOULD JESUS DO?

The third step in our program to accessing the character of God in our lives is knowledge. We are encouraged by Peter to add knowledge to faith and to moral excellence.

Remember when you were a little girl and you made a new friend whom you dearly loved? You just couldn't get enough of each other; you would spend the night at each other's homes, giggle at the same time, read the same books over and over and over again, and hold hands with the innocence of childhood. You were just getting to know this new friend and you couldn't wait to spend time together!

It is pure delight to picture Jesus as your very best friend and to bask in His presence at every moment possible. You should seek Him out from early morning until late at night. Ask Him all of your questions and then take time to listen to what He has to say. Become well acquainted with the Father and with His Son, Jesus Christ. When you truly *know* Him, start asking yourself the provocative question, "What would Jesus do?" This question has the potential to become more than just a catch-phrase of the day in your life. This cultural idiom may soon become your lifeline to accessing the character of God.

"And in your knowledge, self-control, and in your self-control, perseverance, and in your perseverance, godliness . . ." (2 Peter 1:6).

THE BANE OF MY EXISTENCE

Self-control! AH-H-H-H-H! The bane of my existence! There are so many areas of my life that seem to be out of control on a daily basis—spending habits, eating habits, attitudes, my house is a mess, the laundry is never done in a timely manner, the weeds need some attention in the garden, busyness is strangling the life out of me. It never ends, does it?

I am learning that self-control may not be as hard as I have made it out to be. Rather than dreading the daily disciplines of godliness, I have narrowed it down to this proverb: *I need to do what I know that I should do.* That doesn't seem too difficult, does it? Perhaps I need to take it one step further and realize that when I *know* the right thing to do and yet I do not *do* the right thing, that is blatant sin in my life (James 4:17). Could I perhaps liken it to sticking my tongue out in the face of God?

Only *I* have the power to control my tongue and my heart. Only *I* can bring my spending habits and eating habits into submission. *I* can only do this when *I* am renewing myself in the spirit of my mind on a daily basis (Ephesians 4:23). *I* can only do this when *I* put on the new self, which has been created for me in righteousness (Ephesians 4:24). When *I* submit my out of control nature to His control, it takes all of the pressure off my weaknesses and allows me to lean into His great strength. No longer is it the burden of self-control but it is the freedom of God-control!

NEVER, NEVER GIVE UP!

Perseverance is an outdated, archaic word in our society that smacks of the hard-knock life. Perseverance is not nearly as bad as you think it is when you realize that perseverance is a divine strategy to deliver you from emotion-based living. God always has a better idea than we do. When our best idea is to give up, His perfect plan is to hold our hand and help us finish with strength. Perseverance is enduring patience that calls us all to just hang in there . . . one more day. There are only milliseconds between those who win and those who lose the race, or worse yet, those who give up altogether. There is barely a millimeter of difference between those who finish strong and those who are only yards from the finish line gasping for breath and refusing to go on.

Will you be one who is known for never seeing a task to its end because you became too tired or merely lost interest? Or will you be one who knows the value of perseverance and the reward with which it will crown your life? Count me in . . . I am going to finish well and finish strong. I will never give up in dealing with my emotions or in being a better wife or in giving Him control or in accessing His character. I will never give up!

A WHIFF OF HEAVEN

The sixth-step in our call to access the character of God is that we are to embrace godliness. This is a pretty tall order for us who have lived our entire existence in a world that is tattered and torn by the winds of sin and the storms of selfishness. At our very best, we might be a noble piece of humanity but to be like God?! How is it even possible?

Godliness is only possible because He empowers you to be more than you could ever be on your own and to do more than you could even dream with His creative fingerprint on your life. You have the God-given potential of acting like God acts, talking like God talks, of feeling what God feels. This is a rare and priceless call: to live up to the family name and to have the aroma of heaven upon your life. When others observe your life, they should be observing God in you. The world should not see a hollow shell of religious platitudes or a wolf in sheep's clothing, but rather the radiance of heaven should explode from every pore in your body. You are called to live a life of God-likeness while on earth. This is not legalism . . . this is freedom at its finest!

"And in your godliness, brotherly kindness and in your brotherly kindness, love . . ." (2 Peter 1:7).

JESUS JUST WANTS YOU TO BE KIND

Step seven just may have the greatest capability of allowing you to place your emotions in their proper perspective. I can personally guarantee that when your life is over and you call to remembrance all of your accomplishments, all of the books that you have read, all of the places that you have visited, all of the degrees that you have earned, and all of the money that you have acquired, you will yearningly think to yourself, "I should have spent more of my life focusing on step number seven."

If you are focused on being kind to others, the selfishness of your emotional state will fade away into an embarrassing remembrance of childhood immaturity. When someone wrongs you, just be kind. When you are impatient with the sales clerk, your three-year-old or the neighbor's dog, just be kind. Instead of giving your husband the silent treatment, fix him his favorite meal. When your mother-in-law threatens to come and visit for a three-month stay, brandish out your best sheets for her bed and let her have a date with your husband! When your best friend sets you up for a blind date with a total loser, send her a dozen long-stemmed roses!

Kindness is one of the most practical ways in which we are called to exhibit the character of Christ in the world. Whenever one of my children came home from school and were upset with a classmate or with a teacher for what they interpreted as mistreatment, I would pray with the wounded child and then together we would plan a way for my child to bless that guilty, but forgiven, person the next day. The Bible says that we are to bless those who curse us and I believe that when we bless others, the blessing will come back upon us! Most of us are kind to the people whom we love the most and who are kind to us, but the Gospel calls us to love our enemies and pray for those who persecute us. Do not turn this theology into a mere philosophy but make it practical and life changing. Do not go to bed any night of your life unless you have been kind to someone who has mistreated you!

Maggie and Kevin, two of our dear college friends, have been married for over twenty-eight years and have raised four amazing children. Maggie and Kevin travel around the world teaching Christian marriage principles and child-rearing techniques. They find great purpose in preparing young couples for marriage or in attempting to save marriages that are heading for divorce court.

Maggie and Kevin received a phone call from one of their pastor friends who requested that they spend some time counseling the head elder and his wife from his church. Maggie and Kevin readily agreed and prayed fervently that God would give them wisdom and discernment as they advised this desperate couple.

After several weeks of counseling this head elder and his wife and then spending time with their hurting children, it became clear to Maggie and Kevin that this man, this supposed spiritual giant, was abusing his family emotionally. This purported "man of God" had a problem with his tongue, which was complicated with his angry, nearly violent, personality.

One evening, as this couple sat in Kevin and Maggie's living room for yet another counseling session, the religious man put his head in his hands and started to cry, "I just want to be the priest of my home! I just want to be the priest of my home!"

Maggie spoke in wisdom and with witty candor when she replied to his spiritual effusiveness, "Marvin, God just wants you to be kind. Forget about being the priest of your home until you learn to be kind to your wife and to your children."

Jesus just wants you to be kind. He wants you to be kind in every situation to every person on every single day. When in doubt, be kind. When you are filled with anger and smoke is flaring out of your nostrils, be kind. When someone mistreats you or your children, be kind. Even when someone does not deserve it, be kind. As Christians, we are kind not because others deserve it but because the Bible commands it!

WHAT THE WORLD NEEDS NOW

It always comes back to love, doesn't it? There is no more valuable commodity this side of heaven than the love that God has showered on us and calls us to give to others in generous amounts.

When we show anger and spit out impatience towards people, we are only stirring up strife both in their lives and in ours. But, when we die to self and act in love, it covers all of our mistakes and all of our shortcomings (Proverbs 10:12).

Our love for one another must never settle into mediocrity or sadly evolve into toleration mentality but our love for the people that Christ has wisely placed into our lives, is to be fervently expressed. It is fervent love that will help to erase the painful effects of hurt and disappointment (1 Peter 4:8).

You must realize that God has strategically placed you with a group of people so that you may all be challenged to walk in love and talk in love. When life gets messy, it is time to put away the psychology textbooks and turn off *Dr. Phil* and just dive headfirst into an attitude of full-blown, demonstrative love.

I have a lovely friend whom I admire deeply and whose walk with the Lord never ceases to amaze me. As we were having a heart-to-heart discussion not long ago, she was telling me about two of her dearest friends with whom she had shared a friendship since elementary school. They have literally done life together—have shared the years of early marriage, raising children, the empty nest, and now the senior years. These two friends had done something that disappointed her greatly and she said to me, "I don't believe that I will ever go anywhere with them again. I just need some new friends."

I looked into her sweet face and said, "Maybe they need you more than you need them. Maybe it's time to turn up your love not turn your back on it."

The world needs our love. The world needs us to exhibit true Christianity, to come out of our emotional despondency, and to model the love of heaven to this fallen world.

"For if these qualities are yours and are increasing, they render you neither useless nor unfruitful in the true knowledge of our Lord Jesus Christ. For he who lacks these qualities is blind or short-sighted, having forgotten his purification from his former sins. Therefore, brethren, be all the more diligent to make certain about His calling and choosing you; for as long as you practice these things, you will never stumble" (2 Peter 1:8-10).

If you truly follow this eight-step program and are committed to working diligently at accessing the very character of God in your life, you will never stumble in any area of your life. This providentially includes the area of your emotions. When you are focused on connecting with the character of God and then expressing His character to your world, staying in the chains of emotional bondage will seem as important to you as a game of childhood tiddlywinks. As you practice the eight-step program, you will see little victories in your life, then medium victories, and before you know it, by His strength you will know that your life is on glorious display as you exhibit the joy of His presence to the world!

Chapter Eight

A Quiet Spirit

Telling Yourself to Shut Up!

Most of my regrets in life have come from my inability to keep my mouth shut, to reserve my opinions to myself, and to maintain my emotions within some healthy boundaries! When I think of the character assassination that I have committed because of my pride issues I am woefully ashamed. When I am reminded of the little lives that I have wounded with my lethal weapon of a muscle that lies between my pearly whites, I bow my head and repent. The only times when I have come close to hating myself and the person that I have become, is after I have said entirely too much in an opinionated, willful manner at a resonating pitch known as forte.

QUIET YOURSELF

I have five amazing children—they are absolute aces in any mother's heart. The best part of my life has been raising these five unique individuals to be world changers for Christ and His kingdom. I have loved watching all of their distinct personalities develop, their talents increase exponentially due to training and discipline, and also to observe the different types of friends that they have chosen. Their differences are only eclipsed by their similarities. After all, each one of them boasts the same last name for now—McLeod; and all five children have been raised by two parents who love each one of them unconditionally and wholeheartedly.

As much as I have enjoyed observing their uniqueness, I think that it has been their sameness that has been most miraculous. Each one has been a cuddler as an infant and has been what we affectionately dubbed a "hold-me-baby." It was always a bittersweet day when they tumbled out of my arms into their own mobility and I realized that their first step of independence had begun.

When they were newborn babies, I was the only one who could quiet them. It might take hours of rocking and singing a sweet lullaby, but eventually they would relax in their mama's tired arms. As they grew, they learned to quiet themselves and with each child, a different method would work. For our firstborn, it was a pacifier of one particular type and description that we treasured like pure gold! For our second born, it was a wind-up teddy bear that played, *Jesus Loves Me!* Jordan, our third, was best quieted by a particular position in his crib and for Joy, our first daughter, it was that infamous thumb. Joni Rebecca, the baby of them all, had to sleep with a light blue blanket that she named "Ga-Ga" before she was old enough to really speak.

As these babies grew into toddlers, different methods worked as they outgrew the ways of infancy. No longer was it a pacifier that brought peace but it was a book read every night by Daddy. The teddy bear was exchanged for a bedtime snack and the thumb became obsolete in comparison to a backrub by Mom.

PRECIOUS IN THE SIGHT OF GOD

How do you quiet yourself? What brings comfort to you? You must learn to quiet yourself if you want joy more than you desire emotional ventilation. A quiet spirit maintains order as well as a well-placed set of priorities in its emotional makeup. A quiet spirit utilizes self-control in the tongue and in the emotions. The paramount goal of the person who has achieved a quiet spirit is the shining reward of peace.

A gentle and a quiet spirit is one of the attributes of our lives that God loves the very most. The Bible tells us that a gentle and quiet spirit is precious in the sight of God (1 Peter 3:3-4). According to the Word of God, there are two things that are precious in the sight of God, one is the death of His godly ones and the other is a gentle and a quiet spirit. God obviously places a high priority on this meaningful characteristic of a gentle and quiet spirit. I long to be precious to God and so even in the most exacting of circumstances, I will learn how to quiet myself and I purpose to respond in a gentle manner.

The world, conversely, has no patience for a person who has cultivated this serene commodity that is precious in the sight of God. Our culture screams at us to yell vociferously in the face of unfair treatment and disappointment. Athletes squawk at referees, teenagers holler at their parents, and politicians shriek at all of us. Sometimes I wonder if we all look, sound, and act like two-year-olds out of control from heaven's point of view.

Our spirits must be quiet and they must also be gentle. In the deepest part of you, where the real you can be found, there must be a gentle place where peace rules and reigns. A gentle spirit is not harsh and is certainly not wayward. A gentle spirit is not sharp nor is it difficult with which to be compatible. It is not intent on demanding its own way but has selfless boundaries. If you refuse to develop a gentle and a quiet spirit, then you will also refuse joy. Joy is never found where there is criticism or selfishness and defiant joy runs the other direction from a fractious or ornery situation.

SH-H-H-H-H-H!

King David, the psalmist, knew something of having to quiet his own soul. He knew that there were just some things in which he should not involve himself because they were too burdensome for him. When faced with a challenge that was formidable, David recounts the fact that he would quiet his soul just like a weaned child rests against its mother. When David quieted himself and put his soul at rest, it was in that place that he would find hope (Psalm 131: 1-3).

It is necessary to learn how to quiet yourself in the Lord. If you are trying to bring rest to your soul from the senselessness of emotional nutrition, you might as well be gobbling empty calories. There is no hope of joy or of having a gentle and a quiet spirit unless you rest yourself *in the Lord*. There is nothing else that has the ability to pacify your out of control spirit but time spent resting in His presence. I sincerely hope by now that you have outgrown gobbling down chocolate, the momentary thrill of boundless spending, and reading the latest cheap romance novel as a means of quieting yourself.

Have you ever spent time with someone who just does not know how to be quiet? When this loquacious, perpetual motion machine calls on the telephone, you know that this one-sided conversation may last an entire hour or more. If you have coffee with Chatty Cathy, you will smile and nod your head until you feel like one of those bobble-head dolls with glassy eyes. People who have never learned how to listen are as annoying as a rainstorm on the Fourth of July!

The next time that you have lunch with a dear friend or call someone on the phone, be tenderly aware of listening rather than talking. You might want to make a point only to ask them questions and resolve not to respond in anyway that requires more than one sentence. Did you know that sometimes it is more important to tell yourself to "Shut up!" than it is to be a babbling, jabbering, long-winded motor mouth who is cognizant of only your own point of view?!

COME OVER AND SIT A SPELL

The practical side to this spiritual principal is one that has fed my spirit in miraculous ways. How do you rest in the Lord? You read your Bible every day and linger over every word. You memorize the Word of God and select verses that speak to your heart in your current circumstances. You listen to praise and worship music from the time the sun comes up in the morning until it goes down in the evening. As often as you are able, you sing along with the music! Whenever I worship the Lord, it evokes a sense of wonder in my life that He actually thinks I am precious to Him! If you struggle with having a harsh spirit, it is of vital importance to cultivate an active prayer life. Let me challenge you not to pray for yourself for one entire month. During this month, only pray for others and spend time in thanksgiving. You will marvelously discover, at the end of this experimental month, that your rough edges have been smoothed away. You will no longer ferociously be dogging every emotional outrage in your life. Quiet yourself in the Lord.

Craig's grandmother McLeod was a lovely, Southern woman who had lived a dreadful life. She had been married to the town drunk who had physically abused her and the nine children that they shared. It is a sad fact that when her husband died, her life improved immensely. Lillian McLeod was known for attending the high school baseball games with a lawn chair, going out to lunch with her seven sisters, and watching the Atlanta Braves every time they were on television. Whenever she saw that we were across the street at Craig's parents' house, she would come out on her modest front porch, wave her apron, and "yoo-hoo" me across the street. By that time, she would have set her weary bones down in the porch rocking chair and would always greet me with the words, "Carol, why don't you come over and sit a spell?"

Do not let "sitting a spell" become an archaic practice in your modern life. About once every three months, I try to set aside a day for nothing but studying the Bible, praying, and worshipping. I plan this day around the schedule of my family and when I know that they will be occupied the entire day, I relax in the presence of the Lord. I do not put a load of laundry in, cook supper, or even straighten up around the house. Did you know that there are more important things in life than an immaculate home? An immaculate spirit is one of those priceless commodities!

SUNDAY IN YOUR HEART!

God's will for your life is for you to set aside a time of rest. He is eternally wise and He knew that we would never be able to cope with all of the loathsome issues of life without a time of rest in His presence (Hebrews 4:9). A Sabbath rest in our life while on earth is the practice of quieting yourself and finding a deep place of peace within your soul. This fulfilling interlude comes only when you hope in God and not in your tongue. You will experience this leisurely quietude when you let go of your emotional idols and remember that your life is not about you. You will find a Sabbath rest when you walk in the Word and sing for joy! A tranquil, quiet refreshment will follow after you align yourself with a mentor or a spiritual accountant and then choose to be a woman of moral purity. Even God, Who never grows weary or tired, rested from His work after the six days of creation (Hebrews 4:10). If God desired rest, then certainly so should we.

The Bible says that we are to work hard to enter the rest of God! That almost sounds like an oxymoron, doesn't it? How do you work hard to enter rest? It takes diligence to set aside the needful time that will give you a glorious vacation from your emotion-based living. The devil does not want you to have a time of repose in the presence of God and one of the devil's greatest tools today is the art of distraction. You will think of 1,472,968 things to do before you can set time aside just to enjoy the pleasure of His company! Nothing on that endless list of distractions guarantees to bring rest and joy to your soul—you must work hard to enter His rest. It is not an easy place to be but it is the best place to be! If you choose not to enter this place of recess from the demands of life, you might fall into sin (Hebrews 4:11).

It is on this holiday from your foolish emotional sustenance that the Word of God is able to do a deep work in your heart. When you love Him enough to spend time in His presence and when you are so desperate for joy that you will come to a screeching halt in other areas of your life, the Word of God is able to do open-heart surgery on you. The Word will separate in your life what is good and what is not good. The Word will cut away the fleshly desires and attitudes that are not pleasing to Him. This time in His presence will reveal to you the difference between your desires and His desires. It is in the place of quiescence that I am able to allow Him to judge the thoughts and intents of my weary heart (Hebrews 4:12).

Jesus knows what it is like to be tempted emotionally and to want to lash out in anger and in disappointment. Jesus knows the necessity of controlling His frustration and His impatience because He was tempted in all respects that we are tempted and yet He did not sin. The power that Jesus Christ accessed in order to walk in emotional victory is at your very disposal! You can be confident that when you draw near to His throne room of grace that He will be there to help you! When you ask for a quiet spirit, He will quiet the storm in your soul. This is not a one-time opportunity for a sold-out event! You can come to this quiet place of His presence whenever you need Him the most (Hebrews 4: 15-16)!

"I Am Woman—Hear Me Roar" should definitely not be the theme song of your heart and your spirit. When we attack a situation with an avalanche of words and emotional volume, we are negating the power of prayer to change the situation. A quiet and gentle spirit always turns to prayer as a first choice and not as a last resort. If you desire to be truly heard in the throne room of God, then you will cultivate a gentle and quiet spirit. What captures the attention of God is not what is endorsed by the mores of modern society. It is time . . . it is past time . . . to crawl up on His lap and just sit a spell. Leave your agenda at the door and enjoy the sheer relaxation found only in His presence.

Chapter Nine

Who Created Gnats in the First Place?

How to Handle An Offense

The wonder of North Carolina in the summertime! Long, hot days on which to ride your bike down an endless dirt road . . . the sun beating fiercely on your back as you work in the flower garden . . . the leisurely delight of sitting on the front porch and drinking a tall, cool glass of decidedly Southern sweet tea. Firefly nights and flower-blazing mornings! Sidewalk chalk with no remorse . . . baseball games that last long into the evenings. Devouring a watermelon still warm from the garden . . . letting the butter from a fresh piece of corn on the cob drip all the way down your chin . . . and savoring the sweet chill of homemade strawberry ice cream. Life doesn't get any better than this . . . except . . .

Except . . . for one minor intrusion into that celebrated season . . . that two-bit infraction which is very minor in size but not in effect. The miniscule encroachment of which I speak is none other than the dreaded GNAT!

The McLeod family is unashamedly addicted to summertime. When the sun starts to peak out from behind those springtime clouds that signal the end of winter, we are out there in the yard! Picking up trash, clearing out gardens, setting up the picnic table and badminton set seems almost as exciting as Christmas morning to us. When the boys were younger, we used to eat three meals a day outside just because we never seemed to get enough of sunshine on our faces. Christopher loved summer only until the evening hours approached and then he began to dread the onslaught of the infamous North Carolina gnat.

Christopher seemed to draw the gnats to his freckle-infested face like flies to honey. He would swat at them, beat them, run away from them, try to stomp on them, but nothing seemed to work. One evening, while he was trying to lick an ice-cream cone and annihilate gnats at the same time, he just couldn't take it any longer and blurt out, "Why did God have to create these pesky old gnats anyway?"

Being the herculean homeschool mom that I was, I calmly and academically replied, "Well, honey, I am sure that gnats are a part of some other useful insects' food chain. I know that God made gnats for a very particular reason!"

Later that evening, Christopher and I escaped the torment of these troublesome creatures and took the "G" Encyclopedia to the living room couch. I easily found the word "gnat" and we settled down for a bedtime science lesson. There were several great pictures of gnats, the scientific genus and species name for this troublesome creature followed by this one simple sentence: "There is no known scientific reason for the existence of gnats."

Boy! Was my theological bubble burst! No known reason for gnats! How can that be?! God certainly has a reason for everything that He created, doesn't He?

We decided to read further in our out-dated encyclopedia and what we found was nothing short of amazing and discouraging. *"The only desire that an adult female gnat has is blood and she will seek this from any mammal that she can find with people being her favorite target. Though not particularly fast fliers, gnats are hard to kill because they are elusive and persistent. Swatting at them will rarely get them to leave and usually you will have to leave the immediate area if you wish to get relief."*

THE VIOLENT NATURE OF A GNAT

Some of you may want to skip this chapter because it may not apply to you. (Yea! Right!) If you have never been hurt, offended, wounded, or dented by other's opinions, words, actions, or inactions, then you have my permission to read ahead. Do not waste any more time in this chapter because you are truly an invulnerable piece of humanity. For the other ten million of you, let's learn how to handle an offense.

Handling an offense is an imperative area to cover when dealing with the precious commodity of joy. We allow our joy to be violently stolen from us, ripped from our very grasp, by mere gnats! This gnat has no power over your life, there is no venom in its sting or slicing power in its tongue. A gnat does not have the capability to leave even a pinhead sized prick in the issues of your heart. However, when someone insults us or offends us, we allow this merely troublesome gnat to leave a gaping wound accompanied by a monstrous loss of blood and excruciating pain.

Why does this happen? Why can't we just slough off the bothersome nature of the gnats in our lives? There is one simple reason why we are crippled beyond mobility when offended—you think your life is all about you. Repeat after me loud and clear, "My life is not all about me!" Because you have fooled yourself into believing that the earth no longer revolves around the sun but on the day of your birth the vast magnitude of our planet began revolving around little ol' you, you are easily offended by minor issues and you do not guard your joy effectively.

THE LITMUS TEST OF LOVE

The Bible teaches that love is not easily offended or provoked (1 Corinthians 13:5). How easily you are offended just may be the litmus test of your love for someone because if you truly love someone then you will not be easily offended.

Every person alive comes in contact with gnats—people who are troublesome and want nothing more than to suck the blood from your life. These people are persistent and pervasive and the only way that you can afford yourself some relief is to leave the area.

There will always be people who take pleasure in roughing up your emotions but as Christians, we need to be the kind of people who literally defy the power of an offense. Our guiding principal in spending our years as heavenly ambassadors on earth should be that we choose to love deeply in the face of offensive people and hurtful words.

My father often quoted the familiar axiom, "It takes two to fight." Guess what? If you do not retaliate then there will be no battle. If you respond to someone's wounding words with a blast of love then you will win before the skirmish has even started. Now that's a strategy for victory—and for joy!

AN ENGLISH LESSON

The word "offended" has four distinct meanings. The first meaning is "to make bitter" which implies that an outside force has the power to make you into a bitter person. I don't like the sound of that, do you?

The second definition for the word "offended" is "to rouse to anger" which once again implies that someone else has the audacity to make you into an angry person. That still doesn't sound good to me, does it to you?

The third definition of the word "offended" is even more disturbing! This time, the dictionary tells me that the word "offended" clearly signifies "to stir up what is evil in another." So, when someone offends you, this person has the power to stir up what is evil in you!

If I have a problem with anger or with past wounds or hurts or childhood issues and then someone is unkind to me, they have the potential of stirring up that past wound. Unfortunately, people can be unkind both knowingly and unknowingly. If I have unresolved issues in my heart, when someone is unkind to me or to someone that I love, I will become embittered, offended, or provoked.

The interesting aspect of this verb "offended" is that it is not an active verb but a passive verb. An active verb is one in which the subject is doing the action or causing the action to happen. A passive verb is one in which the action happens to the subject because the subject is not causing the action. This gnat-like verb "offended" by its very nature implies that you are not in control but that someone else is controlling you!

The fourth and final definition of the word "offended" is yet another unhappy explanation: "to become sharp like a weapon." You become a weapon of mass destruction when you allow someone to offend you. Women, let's be honest here; if the shoe fits, then wear it! The last time that you were offended, how did you act? The last time that your husband forgot to take out the trash or burped in public, what was your response? I hope that you smiled gently and then responded quietly, "I love you so much. There is absolutely nothing you could do that could stifle my unconditional love for you!" Most of you, unfortunately, turned your back in a huff, gave him the silent treatment for the next three days, and growled whenever he walked into the room. The last time that your girlfriend forgot your birthday or mentioned that you were gaining a little bit of weight, I hope that you wrote her a note telling her how much you appreciate her friendship and set a date for lunch. Most of you, however, either cried yourself to sleep or thought things that I cannot repeat on paper!

It is time for the women who know Jesus Christ as their Lord and Savior to arise in one mighty chorus and sing out at the top of their lungs, "I will not be offended!" You will rarely—if ever—hear me say the words, "I was offended." It is just not part of my vocabulary and I refuse to buy into yet another of Satan's devices to steal my joy. I try always to be the bigger person and to give someone else the benefit of the doubt. One of my core values in life is that I disallow any offense to enter my heart and I find great pleasure in dodging Satan's bullets of offense. I have come to realize that there is greater value in loving someone than in allowing them to offend me. I know that if I can keep strong and true in my love for them, I will not even notice the times that they act ornery or contrary (1 Peter 4:8).

CHRISTIANITY AT ITS FINEST HOUR

When someone does offend you, and it should not happen often, there are two practical ways to deal with this offense. The first thing that you should do is to diligently look for an opportunity to bless the offender. Send a note, make a meal, or look for an opportunity to speak highly of them in public. The one virtue that makes us different from the world is the way that we respond in love to our enemies and to those who have wrongfully offended us. We are to bless the people who have caused the offense and to love them wholeheartedly. Christianity at its finest hour is when someone is cruel to you and yet you choose to love with a smile on your face.

The Bible teaches that when we love our enemies and pray for those who persecute us we are acting like sons and daughters of our Father Who is in heaven. It's part of the family heritage that we are not easily offended and that we choose to bless those who curse us (Matthew 5:44-45). You will be living up to the family name when you are kind to those who do not have a kind bone in their body and have made it their goal in life to make you miserable. When we choose to be extravagant in our love for people who are rough around the edges, we are looking a whole lot like our Dad.

LOVE FINDS A WAY THROUGH

I was offered my dream job—it was the chance of my young lifetime! I had prayed for this door to open and I had to pinch myself to believe that I was really at the right place at the right time. I thought I had surely "arrived" and that my life was going to start on a new, perfect course.

I met everyone in the office on my first day at work and they couldn't have been nicer to me, the new girl from the North. They greeted me with a magnolia leaf in their mouths and offered to do anything at all to help me make a smooth transition.

The second day at work, I noticed some minor friction between some of the staff but I knew that everyone didn't get along all the time and this was to be expected. By my third day at my dream job, I realized that I had just entered the battlegrounds for World War III and that I was caught in the cross-fire. One employee, especially, made it her goal in life to patronize, demean, and humiliate me at every chance that came her way. When the president of the corporation was in the room, Nancy was as sweet as molasses to me but the minute he left, she became the wicked witch of the west!

I prayed for Nancy every day before I left for work in the morning and again every day all the way home in my little orange Volkswagen. I begged God to help me show my love for her in practical ways. What in the world could I have done to deserve this treatment? I knew that I was naïve but I wasn't stupid and I very much wanted to do something, anything at all, to fix the situation. Craig and I prayed for Nancy and talked about what I could do to assuage the situation.

I started to look for every opportunity that I could to bless Nancy or to encourage her or make her job just a little easier. I told her that she looked especially nice one day and invited her to go to lunch with me the next. Nancy just loved chocolate so I would bring homemade brownies into work or some days offer to make the post office run for her.

One afternoon when we were both in the same room, I tried to strike up a conversation with her as we accomplished some mundane tasks. Nancy looked at me and said, "You really don't get it, do you? I don't want to tell you how my weekend was. I don't want to exchange pleasantries with you. All I want is for you to leave me alone." (Except she didn't say it quite as nicely as that!)

Nothing worked. Nothing at all. I remember coming home from work one rainy, autumn afternoon and weeping to Craig, "Love does not always find a way through! It just doesn't."

Craig encouraged me not to give in to my emotional frustration but to keep praying and to keep blessing and to believe for God to bring a miraculous breakthrough.

Two years at my supposed dream job passed by quickly when I found out that I was pregnant. The nesting instinct hit me immediately and I could not wait to leave the battlefield of office intensity for the true calling of my life—motherhood. My relationship with Nancy had settled into a strained coexistence of Pollyanna and Darth Vader. On my last day at the office, Nancy called me into her office and closed the door. I sat there in fear and trembling hoping that the trauma of the moment wouldn't leave lifetime scars on my unborn child.

Nancy held a piece of tissue in one hand as she started to cry but reached out to me with her free hand, "Carol, I hated you from the moment that I laid eyes on you. You are from the North and I am from the South. I couldn't understand a word that you said to me. You are white and I am black. You have a husband who loves you and I have a husband who cheats on me. Now, you are pregnant and I have been told that I will never have children. I am sorry that I have been so mean and bitter toward you but I wanted to see if I could break you down. I wanted to see if this Christianity thing was for real and I found out that it was. Will you pray for me before you leave?"

LET IT GO!

Love always finds a way through. It might take two weeks or two years or two decades but the love of Christ is able to break through the toughest heart and the coldest soul.

I find great joy in making a project out of unlovable people. I challenge myself to find out exactly how much love I can give to the scratchiest person in my life. Challenge yourself to be better than you can humanly be and to rely on the love of Christ to love a difficult person through you. When God sends a fractious person into your life, it is not to frustrate you, steal your joy, or for you to run the other way but it is for you to rely on the love of God to splash out of your heart and into their lonely life. If you allow testy people to rob you of your right to bask in the joy that His presence guarantees, you will live a life tormented by other's personalities.

Recently, I have to admit, that I was in a situation in which I had to fight off a spirit of offense. I was with an extremely amiable woman who loved the Lord with her whole heart. Within the space of about two hours she said three unkind things to me that just cut me to the core. I would just pick myself off the ground concerning her berating remark when wham! Here flew another one out of her disapproving mouth. I had a choice: to become embittered or to become better. I had the choice of letting it go or letting it simmer. I could choose to smile sincerely and continue to converse with her or withdraw (rightfully so, I might add) and refuse any more interaction with her. I had the choice to insult her in return or to say something that would bless her tremendously. As she continued to rattle away, I prayed and asked my loving Father for the strength to LET IT GO! Will I ever confront this person about the unnecessary pain that she cause me? I don't know if I will . . . but probably not. It actually does not matter whether or not I ever tell her how she made me feel. What matters is that it no longer hurts when I think about our conversation and that when I forgave her, I forgave completely. I sent her a kind letter and thanked her for our time together and for her insight on several subjects. I believe that I am a healthier person because I did not wallow in her weaknesses but I allowed the strength of Christ to empower me.

NO EXCUSES

"Summing up: Be agreeable, be sympathetic, be loving, be compassionate, be humble. That goes for all of you, no exceptions. No retaliating. No sharp-tongued sarcasm. Instead, bless,—that's your job to bless. You'll be a blessing and also get a blessing" (1 Peter 3:8-9 The Message Bible).

This is a no excuse Scripture. Do you think that these verses apply to everyone else and not to you? Of course not! Now, think of the person who bothers you so much that you cannot stand it. Think of the person who is like fingernails on the chalkboard of life. Now, think of a way to bless that person! Can you take this person out to your favorite restaurant? Or buy them a great new book or CD. Offer to keep their children or run errands for them.

Fix a meal and drop it off or send them flowers. This is God's will for your life and it is a shortcut on the pathway to joy! If you will learn to bless those who drive you crazy and love the nearly unlovable then God has a blessing in store for you and the name of the blessing is JOY!

Have you been praying for God to show you what His perfect will for your life is? This is it! This is God's perfect will for your life right now today! It is contained in these two authentic verses from 1 Peter. God's will for your life is to bless those who offend you, encourage those who insult you, and speak positively of those who speak negatively of you. What would happen in your life if you really did live by the Bible? What would happen if you put into practice every precept of living that Christ died for? Your world would be filled with pure, unadulterated, extravagant joy!

Craig and I and our five children had lived in North Carolina for sixteen sun-kissed, heavenly years when God called us to move to New York. It was very painful for me to say good-bye to the women who had prayed for me through miscarriages, loved my children unconditionally, blessed me during hard financial times, listened to my heart through my tears, and had held my hands as I sent my boys off to college. Every final moment spent with each friend was a tender moment and filled with the ripe possibility of tears or laughter.

My last Sunday morning at church was especially agonizing as I looked at everyone for one last time and tried to memorize each dear face. One woman, Katherine, pulled me aside and said that she wanted to speak to me. She said that she wanted to ask me to forgive her for ill feelings that she had against me since the day that we met. She said that she had never liked me, that she had envied my life, and resented my gifts and abilities. Katherine wanted to know if I would forgive her for all of those heretofore unspoken feelings that she had harbored in her heart.

Of course I would and could forgive her! But it was causeless for her to share those emotions with me because *I never knew that she felt that way.* I had been convinced for fifteen years that we were friends and that we genuinely enjoyed one another's company. This was really an issue that she needed to settle with God and not with me. Do not spew your emotional carelessness on other people. You need to do business with God and leave others out of the conversation.

One of the greatest weapons of warfare that we hold this side of heaven is the high-powered weapon of forgiveness. You are a powerful woman when you forgive and just let it go. Our call is not to retaliate but to be kind. Our new nature in Christ is forbidden to hold bitterness but is encouraged to be tenderhearted and loving. We are to respond to all of life's situations in the same manner that God treated us—He forgave us thoroughly and completely.

When someone offends you, it just may be a setup by God! God trusts you to love this person and to care tenderly for them. God trusts you to keep the minor things minor and to bring them to a place of health and stability. It is not God's will that someone mistreats us, but it is His will that you act like a true Christian towards this individual.

If you ever wonder, "Should I confront this person? Should I tell them how I feel?" My rule of thumb is always . . . no. First, I forgive, then I bless, then I befriend with the Father's great love. The joy that fills my heart is nothing short of miraculous when I obey the Word of God and do life His way!

Chapter Ten

An Epidemic of Emotional Proportions

Worry and Fear

There is a vicious disease in America today that is tormenting women and then is attacking their families. This cancer is relentless in its pursuit of innocent women and once it has grasped its spindly fingers around your mind it then travels to your heart until it consumes your entire life. This plague is more than a mere malady and if it comes in contact with any part at all of your emotional system you will find it nearly impossible to break free of its loathsome grasp.

This dreaded disease is none other than *worry* and, unfortunately, is always accompanied by its twin brother whose name is *fear*. Worry and fear ... why do some women deal with these tormentors nearly every day of their life? How does a child become a fearful child? Some people are tormented to the extent that they are not able to lead normal lives and are crippled by phobias.

A phobia, the dictionary tells us, is a consistent, abnormal, irrational fear of a specific thing or situation. Psychologists and psychiatrists alike agree that most phobias are illogical and are birthed in one's imagination not in reality or fact. The National Institute of Mental Health found that between 5 percent and 22 percent of all Americans suffer from some type of phobia. When compiling a specific study on exactly who is plagued by phobic mental illness, the study clearly showed that women exhibited a disproportionately higher rate of phobias than did men. Agoraphobia, basiphobia, chionophobia, dikeophobia, emetophobia, and the list goes on and on and on.

Why have women, in the American culture, allowed themselves to be paralyzed by irrational fears? Why have Christian women allowed fear to creep into their lives and steal their joy? Why indeed?

SLAYING GIANTS AND DEALING WITH FEAR

David, the intrepid King of Israel—the man who when he was a youth fought off a bear and a lion and then slew the giant Goliath with only a slingshot . . . the man who defeated army after army after army and brought victory to the great chosen nation of God—had a problem with fear and anxiety. David felt as though his insides were turned inside out as he shook with fear. He shuddered from head to foot and literally begged God to allow him to escape from his surroundings. David was afraid of dying and felt that his life was a story of horror. He compared his life situations to a stormy wind that had no end

(Psalm 55:4-9). David entreated God to grant him the ability to fly away as a bird so that he could find a place of peace and quiet away from his fears and worries. God especially takes tender care of birds and feeds them daily—how comforting to know that He loves us far more than He loves birds (Matthew 6:26)!

KITTENS AND BRAIN TUMORS

I believe that fear and worry are not birthed out of insecurity or a lack of confidence. I do not believe that the source of fear is instability or even from a precarious life situation. I believe that *fear* and its sorry partner *worry* are birthed out of their obscene cousin who is known as *pride*. Some might disagree and defend the argument that most people who struggle with fear and worry issues have a problem with a low self-esteem. On the contrary, perpetual worry and consistent fear are simply a lack of trust in the God of the universe Who created you in His image, knows you by name, has numbered the very hairs on your head and has your name imprinted on the palm of His hand. If you cannot put all of your trust in a God like that, then you must have a gargantuan ego if you believe that He is not able to care for you.

I entreated God for many years that I would be a beneficiary of His constant and comforting peace. I was worried and bothered about so many things: our finances, my marriage, the church, our children, the roof on our house, and too many kittens. I would start worrying about having enough money for Christmas in the month of July and then in January would begin to agonize over whether or not we would be able to afford a vacation that year. What if someone stole my children? What if my headache was really a brain tumor? What if our prolific cat had yet another batch of kittens?!

The Holy Spirit delicately led me to a very familiar verse of Scripture and then helped me with the interpretation of it. "The steadfast of mind You will keep in perfect peace because he trusts in You" (Isaiah 26:3). I realized that peace was not something that I should pray for but *peace was a by-product of my trust in God.* I would only enjoy peace when I placed all of my trust in the God Who never fails. The more that I took my eyes off myself and trusted Him, it was to that degree that I would have peace. It became quite simple—greater trust results in greater peace. Even now, I can become consumed with worry or fear when I forget my perspective and think that my problems are too big for even God to solve. That is nothing else but pure, 100 percent pride. If you think that your sin is so great that God cannot forgive you then you have a problem with pride. If you think that your life is so out of control that it is beyond God's power to bring order to your life then the diagnosis is pride. Webster may have many definitions for the word "pride" but I would like to submit this definition to you: You have become bigger than God in your mind and in your heart. If that describes you, no wonder you are a victim of the dread diseases fear and worry! It has attacked your emotional system and you are caught in an epidemic that all started with your ego. People who wallow in fear and worry believe that in all of recorded history, their problems are the only ones that God is not able to take care of. How twisted is that?!

I have the cure for you—take yourself off the throne of your heart and put God back on this place of prominence.

I do believe that most people who struggle with worry and fear also struggle with low self-esteem. However, it is imperative to remember that all self-esteem issues are merely symptoms of a larger problem, which is focusing too much on self and your deficiencies. How you regard yourself contains the evidence of how heavily you lean on your family history and the comparison of yourself to others. Your self-esteem also may reflect a perceived lack of talent or an emphasis on out of control emotions when evaluating yourself and the person whom God created you to be. This preoccupation with self gives birth to worries and fear in every area of your life.

A SLAP IN THE FACE TO GOD

Worry is a slap in the face to God. Did you hear what I just said? Let me say it again just in case you were not listening well . . . *Worry is a slap in the face to God!* Neither worry nor fear is God's will for your life and there is a way that you can victoriously overcome the damage that these two marauders have done in your life.

You must change your thinking starting right now and begin to understand that peace is a by-product of trust. Every time that you hear worry knocking on the back door of your heart and fear ringing the front doorbell simply say, "I trust You, God. There is nothing that is too difficult for You."

After you change your thinking, the second most effective panacea for this disease is to read the Bible every day. The great Korean pastor, Dr. Cho, who has built the largest church in the world, sets aside a few days a month for counseling the people in his church. After listening to their problems for one hour, he makes a notation on a piece of paper, lovingly smiles at the church member and then sweetly asks them to leave. As his counselees leave Dr. Cho's counseling office and then look at the piece of paper, which he has just handed to them, they see that he had written an apparent prescription just like a doctor would write for a patient. On this piece of paper, would be written words similar to this, "Read your Bible 3x a day and spend 5 days at Prayer Mountain." If the problem discussed was extremely large, the prescription might read, "Read your Bible 5x a day and spend 10 days at Prayer Mountain while fasting." Dr. Cho knew that the answer to their phobias was not changing their circumstances but it was changing their perception of their circumstances. The only way that one is able to accomplish this is through the Word of God and time spent in prayer.

SHRINKING VIOLET

Joni, our youngest daughter, has always lived in the shadow of four older siblings who are over-achievers to the extreme. She has watched her sister and brothers bring home spelling bee awards, science fair ribbons, athletic trophies, academic scholarships, and music accolades. They ran faster, had more friends, finished their chores sooner, and did everything better than she did . . . or so she thought. This perception of her imagined deficiencies had caused Joni to be unusually shy and withdrawn. She would only talk to me in public by whispering in my ear and was not able to look anyone in the eye. She was not able to order for herself in a restaurant or speak to adults or children outside of her immediate family.

When Joni turned ten, she realized that most of her friends at church were participating in an extraordinary program known as "Bible Quiz." Children are coached to memorize particular passages from the Word of God and then compete at meets where they are questioned concerning their knowledge. Joni observed the camaraderie and social interaction that her friends were experiencing in this venue and asked us if she could join Junior Bible Quiz.

We immediately said, "Yes!" because we knew the value of hiding God's Word in your heart, but never imagined that God was about to do a miracle in our shrinking violet. We fully anticipated the fact that Joni would do a superb job in memorizing the Scriptures but when she arrived at the places of competition she would sit quietly while others answered. Boy! Were we ever wrong!

Joni took the Bible Quiz world by storm and is one of the top quizzers in the state of New York. Our formerly painfully shy little girl has become a confident young woman with the Word of God firmly hidden in her dauntless heart. She now looks people in the eye and answers their questions with confidence. Joni asks questions and orders for herself in every restaurant. The Word of God has delivered this painfully shy young girl and has transformed her from embracing a life of fear to the confidence of a life of faith. If it worked for Joni, it will work for you. When you immerse yourself in the Word of God, you will be able to relax and know that with God, you are in good hands!

HE IS GOOD AND HE IS GOD!

After you change your thinking and then immerse yourself in the Bible, the third aspect of overcoming worry and fear is to confess every day exactly Who God is. The Lord is your Light and your Salvation—whom shall you fear? The Lord is your Strong Tower and a Shelter in the time of storm. The Lord is the Great Physician, the Mighty Counselor, and the Prince of Peace. He is Love, He is Wisdom, and He is the God of all Hope. He is the Lord of Hosts and He is Your Sanctuary. When you decisively make a confession and acknowledge Who God is and what He is able to do in your life, you will be living a life of great joy!

By now, I hope that you know I am hopelessly in love with the Word of God. The Bible is able to combat your worst fears and your nightmarish worries. If we were sitting across the table from one another perhaps having a glass of iced tea complemented by a bakery fresh cookie, I would read some of my favorite verses of Scripture to you. You see, I am poignantly aware that anything I say will fade away but the Word of God has eternal power to change your impossibilities into reality! I hope that you will not complete this chapter without taking the time to read these beloved Scriptures from the Gospel of Matthew. Please read them—they will change your thinking and therefore, your life!

> *For this reason I say to you, do not be worried about your life as to what you will eat or what you will drink; nor for your body as to what you will put on, is not life more than food and the body more than clothing? Look at the birds of the air, that they do not sow, nor reap nor gather into barns, and yet your heavenly Father feeds them. Are you not worth much more than they?*
>
> *And who of you, by being worried, can add a single hour to his life? And why are you worried about clothing? Observe how the lilies of the field grow; they do not toil nor do they spin. Yet I say to you, Solomon in all his glory clothed himself like one of these. But if God so clothes the grass of the field, which is alive today and tomorrow is thrown into the furnace, will He not much more clothe you? You of little faith!*
>
> *Do not worry, then, saying, "What will we eat or what will we drink? Or what will we wear for clothing?"*
>
> *For the Gentiles eagerly seek all these things for your heavenly Father knows that you need all these things. But seek first His Kingdom and His righteousness and all these things will be added to you. So do not worry about tomorrow for tomorrow will care for itself. Each day has enough trouble of its own."*
>
> Matthew 6: 25-34

Chapter Eleven

The Dance of God in Your Life

The Joy of Destiny

This chapter is about to place the exclamation mark at the end of your plea, "I long for defiant joy!" I hope that by now you believe in joy and that you are firmly convinced that God's will for your life is to become a woman of God filled to overflowing with defiant joy. This certainty of God's nature manifesting itself in your life will create an environment in which joy will become a divine by-product of your human nature. Joy will be as natural to you as breathing and as delightful as eating a piece of gourmet chocolate. Joy will be as easy as humming your favorite song and as soothing as a glass of pink lemonade on a hot summer's day.

Have you ever asked yourself the question, "Who in the world am I?"

Or, perhaps, different questions have become the haunting melody or your life, "Why was I created? Why was I born?"

Maybe your daily question is this, "What is my destiny? Do I even have a destiny?"

The challenge remains in discovering the answer to the ageless question, "What was I placed on this earth to accomplish?"

YOUR DIVINE LOVE AFFAIR

We were all created for a specific reason at a definite time in history. God has a plan for your life and figuring out this plan is vital to bringing His love and His joy to your world. If you had not been created, God would not be able to accomplish His purposes in the world today. The divine plan of God demands that you fulfill what was in His heart when He thought of you. I believe the way that you discover your destiny is by defining what you absolutely love to do.

To what are you devoted? Perhaps it is painting or visiting with people or gardening or writing notes. What are you absolutely passionate about? Maybe you just love studying the Bible or teaching children or playing the piano.

At what do you excel? Possibly listening to people or cooking or cleaning or singing.

If you had an extra two hours every day to invest in any activity that you could choose, what would it be? Would you spend it just hanging out with your family, having coffee with friends, leisurely reading a wonderful book, or perhaps going for a jog in the neighborhood?

What really piques your interest? Maybe you just love making crafts or possibly you are a history buff. Maybe you are just itching to travel or take ballroom dancing lessons.

God made you just the way you are for a reason and He placed within your soul likes and dislikes as well as strengths. He has bestowed upon you talents and gifts and abilities that He has given to no one else alive today.

One of my most vivid childhood memories are those never-ending Sunday evening church services at which a missionary (usually from the dark continent of Africa) would speak. These great men and women of God showed their vivid slides of snakes and of women without proper clothing, or told stories of dreadful diseases and cannibal tribes, or even displayed artifacts of shrunken heads and tribal weapons. As a little blonde girl who had hardly been allowed to even cross the street by herself, I was petrified that God would call me to be a missionary! I used to beg God, while lying on my bed at night, "Please God! I will do anything for you but please don't make me be a missionary!"

The possibility of a life lived far away from home and family with an aboriginal tribe continued to haunt me into my teenage years. One day, a very astute Young Life leader, casually mentioned to me, "Carol, I am sure that God is going to use you to mentor young women. You have a great capacity for speaking and writing and I believe that God has called you to teach the Bible to women." Was I ever relieved! I didn't have to go to Africa to serve God or be used by Him! I could stay in America and do what I loved to do the most—convince others that His ways are best and that the Bible is the most life-changing book ever written!

What do you love to do? I believe that God has placed your gifts, talents, and abilities in you for a reason and that reason is to share His love with the world. Like Moses, take what is in your hand and use it to lead people into His presence!

AN UNPAINTED CANVAS

Before your life even consisted of two tiny cells that came together in your mother's womb, God was intimately acquainted with you and had a perfect and divine plan for every single day of your life. As you grew from two cells, to four, and then to eight, God was orchestrating the entire growth process. He was watching you, with joy in His heart and probably with tears running down His eternal cheeks, as you grew into a baby whose life was an unpainted canvas yet to become a masterpiece. He heard your first infant cries and His heart skipped a beat in anticipation of every song that you would sing and every book that you would write. He watched as your tiny fingers curled around the fingers of the people whom He had chosen to be your parents and He saw the pictures that you would paint with those fingers and the great works that you would play on the piano. Your heavenly Father watched as you smiled for the very first time and He heard all of your laughter that was yet to come and He thought of all of the people to whom your life would bring great joy (Psalm 139:13-18).

When God created you, He was awaiting all of the miracles that He would do through you because His thoughts concerning you were filled with unlimited possibilities and dreams that would come true. When God first thought of you, He realized that His plan would not be complete without you and so He breathed life into your soul at this time in history for a specific plan and purpose. Your joy will never be complete until you discover God's plan for your life and then begin to live your life with His purposes as your compass.

You are God's favorite child (yes, you!) and every time that He looks at you a silly grin is plastered all over His heavenly face. He thinks of you more times every day than there are grains of sand on the ocean shore (yes, I am talking about you!) and when He thinks of you—a song bursts forth in His heart. When you set aside time from your busy schedule to spend time just hanging out with Him, the God of the entire universe dances because you are spending time with Him!

A MORSEL OF HEAVEN'S GRANDEUR

Every child is structured with the genetic makeup of his or her parents. You might be the beneficiary of sparkling blue eyes or two monstrous feet or an ability to let your voice soar in a musical symphony. Children reflect the nature of their parents in looks, health, and talents. God, your heavenly Father, has placed within your soul a piece of His divine nature. There is, deep within your heart, a morsel of heaven's grandeur that you are to live out while on earth. The part of the genetic structure of God that is within you is your destiny!

Perhaps you have been endowed with the mercy of God and so your destiny might reveal itself in the field of medicine or on the mission field or as a social worker. God may have placed His inexpressible love of children within your heart and you will feel most at home while holding children in your lap or in a classroom or volunteering at a children's hospital. You may have the ability that Christ has to communicate effectively and perhaps your destiny is to write books or act on the stage or be a radio host. You may have been given your Father's ability to heal or to counsel or to be a peacemaker.

If you want defiant joy, then you must figure out why you have been created at this time in history. You must discern the piece of heaven that lies planted dormant within your soul and then bring that piece of heaven to glorious life! When you begin to operate in the part of God's character that has been gifted to you and then begin to walk in your destiny, nothing will be able to touch your joy! There will be a spring in your step and a song in your heart and the windows of heaven will be open upon your life.

THE HEAVENLY RED CROSS

Many Christian women today do not believe that their life holds any eternal purpose and although they know that they are born-again and will spend eternity in heaven, they do not believe that God would ever think of using them for anything significant. I know a woman who believes that if God were choosing teams, she would suffer the humiliation of being the very last one chosen. Satan loves to lie to God's family and when Satan lies, he always tells us that we *lack* what God says we have been *given*. If you think that you lack destiny or purpose then you are listening to the lies of Satan that are intended to steal your joy and to keep you from fulfilling the mission of God upon your life.

The Bible says that we all have been given the ministry of reconciliation, which I refer to as the Heavenly Red Cross (2 Corinthians 5:17-18). You are to bring aid or relief to a world of hurting people whose lives have been destroyed by a tidal wave of tragedy. You are called to bind up the broken-hearted and to visit those in prison. God's expectation for your life is that you would take care of widows and orphans, that you would provide financial support for missionaries, and that you would welcome the homeless into your home. Your life is not about your comforts or financial preferences but it is about those whom you are called to serve. The purpose of your calling is not about receiving recognition, a purple heart, or even a standing ovation. The reason that God has placed a piece of heaven in your heart is not so that you would win an Academy Award or even earn a pat on the back but that you would be the beneficiary of the joy that comes from the simple act of service. Receiving a thank you note should not bring joy into your heart nor should having your face on the cover of *Christianity Today*. Joy is a natural result of hearing God's voice, obeying God's voice, and loving a world who has been torn apart by the ravages of war. It is the resolve of heaven that while on earth, during our watch, we meet the needs of the world as much as it is within our power to do so (Proverbs 3:27).

If indeed we have all been called to the "ministry of reconciliation"—what exactly does this ministry mean? To reconcile means to "restore to divine favor or to make a difference." This ministry, which has been lavished upon us with heavenly rewards in sight, means that with every person that you meet—to every life under your influence, to every soul that you touch—you have one goal and one goal alone. There is only one reason why God has placed that person in your life and that is because you have the power to restore each individual to divine favor of your Father and to a covenant relationship with God. The only reason for building relationships while here on earth is to make a difference for Christ and His kingdom!

The reason why God gives you associates at work is not so that you can discuss the latest office dirt around the water cooler but so that you can win them to Christ! The impetus for developing a relationship with your neighbors is not so that they will take care of your dog while you are out of town but is so that you can introduce them to the Prince of Peace! When you receive an invitation to your next high school reunion, do not immediately plan to lose weight, buy a new outfit, or look up the quarterback on the football team from twenty something years ago, but start praying for the acquaintances of your youth and ask God to give you creative ideas how you can share the love of Christ with these golden friends.

You are called to be a difference-maker every day of your life, in every situation in which you find yourself and with every person that you meet. You are called to make their lives just a little bit easier because you are in it. You are to bring more love, more enthusiasm, more joy, and more peace to their world than was there before you arrived. You have the rare and divine privilege of oiling each life that you meet with the joy of His presence!

ARCHIPPUS AND TIDDLYWINKS

Paul, the anointed apostle of the New Testament, had a passion for training young men who were called into the ministry. Paul encouraged these young men to live lives of moral conviction, to stand firm in the face of horrific trials, and to never give up in their resolve to reach people with the message of the Cross. Archippus is mentioned twice by Paul in two books of the New Testament, in both Colossians 4:17 and in Philemon 2. Archippus may have been a Roman soldier who had become a member of the early church or he may have been the son of Philemon. While we do not know exactly who Archippus was, we can discern his weakness. Archippus needed encouragement to finish the task that he had started. He may have been ministering in some capacity and then had grown weary or lazy and the job was not being finished. These are the words of Paul to Archippus nearly two thousand years ago, "Archippus, take heed to the ministry which you have received in the Lord that you may fulfill it" (Colossians 4:17).

Put your name in that Scripture and remind yourself that you are a part of a legacy of believers who were called to fulfill the plan of Christ in each epoch in history in which they lived. It is no small thing to take heed to the ministry to which you have been called and then to fulfill it! This is not some celestial game of tiddlywinks in which you are participating. The lives of men and women for all eternity are at stake as you decide whether or not you will fulfill the ministry to which you have been called.

Like Archippus, we too, are guilty of failing to complete our work for the Lord due to lack of enthusiasm, moral compromise, or just leaving it up to others. You are able to cheerfully encourage the lady at the grocery store when you are having a good day, but if your boss was in a blue funk today and took it out on you, then you take it out on that precious grocery store lady. If you are in a hurry and running late for Bible Study, then you do not take the time to listen to your teenager who was cut from the basketball team that day. If you are suffering from PMS, you are short with your mother on the phone, ignore the elderly lady next door, and blow up at the cashier at the drive-through window. Take heed! Pay attention to your ministry and stop making excuses why you are not able to fulfill it. You have a piece of heaven in your soul and you must express it or your joy will be stripped away from you.

A KICK IN THE PANTS

Do not lose heart or become discouraged as you travel through life and are doing your best to fulfill the ministry that has been so generously given to you (2 Corinthians 4:1). Keep going on in love when no one responds to you—keep praying the prayer of faith even though the answers seem a life-time away—keep serving your family, your church, and the Lord even though you see no results at all. The paycheck that comes from a lifetime of service may not come in the mail until you see your life from a heavenly perspective. The benefit of serving Him today and of loving others for Him is that you will be filled with unexplainable joy and the word "depression" will never again enter your vocabulary!

Do not allow the years of your life to roll by with a vision that is never fulfilled and so this vision becomes merely the haunting echo of your life. Be diligent in your ministry and take seriously the calling of God upon your life. There will be many days when you have to endure hardship but I believe that if you do things the right way then joy will always blossom in abundance in your life!

What is it going to take to fulfill the plans and purposes of God in your life? Some of you may have to go back to school and continue your education while others just need to take the time to revitalize an old resume. Many women need to rearrange their busy-ness so that they have time to include the truly para-mount issues in their lives. Maybe it is just time for you to make the choice to sit down at the piano and write the song that has been playing on the strings of your heart for years. Possibly, like me, it is time for you to set aside time every day to sit before that computer screen until a book that has been hidden in the library of your heart comes to life! I'll bet that most of you just need an old-fashioned kick in the pants!

Do not let your life go by without investing your-self in something greater than yourself. Make your life count for something today and make a difference in the lives of others. Mothers, now is the season to read to your children, play games as a family, make up songs that express your love for the little ones with whom you have been entrusted, go on long walks through rustling leaves, or take the time to sit around the table and make play-dough. You will never have this opportunity again to disciple the world changers who currently live within the four walls of your home. Do not let the years of your children's childhood pass by in one busy blur of mismatched laundry, macaroni and cheese, and school activities.

Wives, you have the potential to make a life-changing difference in the life of your spouse when you turn your marriage into a ministry. Encourage your husband with your words, your actions, as well as your attitudes. Speak kindly of your knight in shining armor in all situations and always make time for romance. Enjoy life together, play tennis, go out for coffee, go to concerts, or go on a missions trip together. I made a tremendous blunder right after our honey-moon—I blinked and when I opened my eyes, I found that I had been married for nearly three decades. Love your spouse extravagantly and fulfill your God-given calling to marriage that is guaranteed to usher an inordinate amount of joy down the aisle of your heart.

Embrace a mission-field mentality concerning your career and the work place where you spend forty hours per week. You are not there only to earn money because as a Christian, you must definitely believe that your job is not your source—God is your Source! Make it your business to know the birthdays of your co-workers, their children's names, and their favorite kind of doughnut. When your workmate is ornery, choose to shower them with kindness; when your business comrades are discouraged, bring the joy of the Lord into their world; when someone in the office needs someone to talk to, do not skirt the issue but take them out to lunch and then pick up the tab!

If you are looking for a place to express your talents you might try to find something to do at church! Imagine that! Serving in your local church! Find just one particular thing to do at church and then do it with excellence and with gusto! However, if you are spending every single night of the week at church, you are doing a great disservice to yourself and to your family. Choose one department at church that needs help and then plant yourself there.

Create a larger existence for yourself than your favorite television show, the last novel that you read, or your credit card balance. The desire of God is that you should be exuberant in sharing the piece of His divine nature that resides in you.

"But none of these things move me, neither do I count my life dear unto myself, so that I might finish my course with JOY, and the ministry, which I have received of the Lord Jesus, to testify the gospel of the grace of God" (Acts 2:24).

Chapter Twelve

A Plumb Line to His Presence

I Will Choose Joy!

After all the chapters have been read and all of the theology has been digested . . . after all your tears have been shed and your heart feels refreshed . . . there remains yet one more question. Will you choose joy? Will you choose to be a defiantly joyful Christian or will you choose to wallow in the mire of depression, bitterness, and perhaps even refuse to forgive? I hope that you will be so relentless in your pursuit of joy that you will not take one more breath without the reality of defiant joy entwining itself in your heart. Do you want joy more than anything else in life?

Do you desire joy more than money or clothes or more than a man? Do you want joy more than a new home, having your own way, or even changing your husband? Are you more fearless in your pursuit of joy than you are in your pursuit of success or of having children or of winning the affection of others?

A PLUMB LINE TO HIS PRESENCE

In historical times, builders or architects did not have the advantage of the modern technical equipment that is at our disposal today. Today, builders use computer graphics, schematics, architectonics, and all types of equipment to aid in building a secure and functional building. However, even during ancient times, those who were building an edifice or structure knew that if the building was not built with a plumb line that the building would be unable stand the test of time. A plumb line is a line or cord having at one end a weight used to determine verticality. This line is directed exactly to the center of the earth's gravitational pull.

A plumb line is referred to in the Bible in the book of Amos when God came to Amos and showed him a plumb line as He was standing beside a vertical wall. God asked Amos what he saw in His hand and Amos said, "Lord, I see a plumb line" (Amos 7:8). God then told Amos that He was setting a plumb line in the midst of His people that very day. God's people had been built according to God's standards and were expected to stay true to those standards. However, the people of God were completely out of plumb when they were tested. God knew that these rebellious people had to be reminded of God's standards and boundaries.

I believe that God has also placed a plumb line in your life that will give your life balance and structure and will keep you going in the right direction. This plumb line will keep you directly in line with God's will for your life and will enable you to build a foundation in your life that will stand the test of time and will stand strong through emotional earthquakes and tempestuous storms. God's will for your life is a plumb line or a tool that will guide you into correct decision making and focus for your life. This plumb line will determine the verticality of your life, which is quite simply how well you touch God. The plumb line is a measuring gauge that calculates the access that your life has to His presence. A plumb line will ensure that your life has a direct connection to the throne room of God so that you will not waste your time on circuitous routes or rabbit trails or even distractions. What is the plumb line of your life? What is the plumb line that will enable you to build a life of defiant joy?

I can tell you what your plumb line is not: it is not designer clothes, or how much you weigh, how much money you make, or the number of stamps in your passport. The plumb line of your life is quite simply your choice. Will you choose joy or not? *If you choose it, then you can have it*! You have a straight line into the presence of God that will enable you to build a life based on the joy that is found there. If you do not choose joy, then your life will be a maze of one dead end after another that only ends in mere happiness.

There is a weight at the end of the plumb line that keeps the plumb line stable and holds it securely in the center of gravitational attraction. Once you choose joy, there must be a weight on the end of your plumb line as well. The weight on the end of the plumb line is a conscious decision to die to self and to worry, to die to depression and selfishness and fear. You must be a desperate woman who so acutely desires joy that every decision you make during your life will be guided by this plumb line: I will choose joy!

DESPERATE WOMEN

You may be one of these desperate women that I have just referenced but you may also wonder, "How do I choose joy?" In practicality, the way that you choose joy is by choosing His presence every hour of every day. When you are desperate for joy you spend every possible hour of your life in the Word of God, in worship, and by cultivating a healthy and purposeful prayer life. The song that reverberates on the keys of your heart is, *I Won't Last a Day Without You!*

The world will try to give you a false weight or balance to tie on the end of your plumb line. Our culture readily admits that building a life on joy is a noble pursuit but the world will endeavor to convince you that the weight on the end does not need to be the death to self and the assassination of emotional nutrition. The ethics of Western society will submit that joy can come through material pleasures or through healthy relationships or financial success or an Ivy League education. The mere thought of this philosophy is an abomination to the Lord because He knows the delight of a just and true weight (Proverbs 11:1).

There is only one just weight and that is time spent in His presence. God is delighted when you decide to spend quality *and* quantity time in His presence. His presence will always change your perspective because you will see things from His heart and not from your emotional disadvantage point.

Will you choose defiant joy? No one can choose it for you but it comes only from your willful determination. When I spend time in His presence I become enraptured with everything that He is and lose sight of everything that I am not.

In the Lord's covenant with Moses in the book of Deuteronomy, the Lord sets before Moses a very specific choice. Moses and the people of Israel are given the choice of life or death and of blessing or cursing. The Lord further tells Moses that if they choose life the blessing will be upon the generations to come (Deuteronomy 30:19). I believe that when you choose joy over depression the blessing will also be on your family for many generations to come. You will be leaving a legacy for your children and grand-children and great-grandchildren that will be more valuable than gold or stocks and bonds.

Will you do life His way with the miracle power of joy? Or will you buy into the compromising prospects of our society? When you choose joy, you are choosing for your household a brand new way to do life. Joshua was given much the same choice as he was leading the people of Israel and he was forced to choose between the heathen gods of the land or the true God of Isaac and Abraham. Joshua emphatically declared publicly for the entire nation to hear, "As for me and my house, we will serve the Lord" (Joshua 24:15). Perhaps it is time for you to make a public confession as well and commence to make a brazen announcement to your family, friends, and co-workers: "I will serve the Lord with all of my choices. I will no longer be in bondage to a negative and critical spirit. I will choose the joy of His presence!"

When you do choose joy, you are choosing a brand new way to do life for your entire household. You will be trumpeting the fact that yours is a home where no longer are voices raised in anger and where people are not allowed to demand their own way. You will be proclaiming that yours is a home where the family members walk in forgiveness and peace and blessing and joy.

When it comes down to it—it is all a choice, isn't it? Reading your Bible every day is a choice that you make. Putting on the whole armor of God and deciding to enrich yourself with a life of worship is a choice, isn't it? Allowing your spirit to rule over your emotions is a choice that you make. Embracing a quiet spirit, refusing to worry, and not carrying an offense is all a choice. It is up to you, after all. Will you choose joy?

I have recently turned fifty-one years old and I know that I have most likely lived over half of my life but of this one thing I am certain: I will choose joy! There is no other way to live that holds any attraction at all for me. I will read my Bible every day no matter how crazy my schedule or how messy my house is. I will be a worshipper every day, every season. I will sing loud and strong. Sometimes, I might sound off-key to you but I am going to keep right on singing my way into joy! I will not make my emotions into ridiculous idols because I am fully aware that my life is not all about me and my desires and preferences. I will have a quiet spirit and will tell myself wisely to "shut up" from time to time. I will trust and not worry and I will not allow anyone to hurt my feelings. I will bless those who offend me. I will serve others with my gifts, talents, and abilities and make the most of every opportunity that I am given. I will choose joy! Will you?

Author Contact Information

Carol McLeod

Founder, Just Joy! Ministries

3210 Southwestern Blvd.

Orchard Park, NY 14127

Phone number: 716-712-0015

Fax number: 716-712-1740

Web site: www. justjoyministries. com

E-mail: carol@justjoyministries. com